Sport Images

FIRST EDITION, FIRST PRINTING, SEPTEMBER 2000

SPORT IMAGES, 7211 WOODROW DRIVE, OAKLAND, CALIFORNIA 94611 USA
TELEPHONE: 510-339-2320 FAX: 510-339-3482
COPYRIGHT ©2000 SPORT IMAGES

ISBN 0-9618712-5-3

THE GOLF BALL BOOK

A Sport Images book by
Udo Machat

Text by Larry Dennis

To that much thought about shepherd,

who may have been the first

to swing a crook at a rock...

We, the golfers of the world, thank you.

And, we forgive you.

CONTENTS

FOREWORD

Most popular athletic sports use a ball to determine the outcome of their contests, from handball, one of the oldest, to basketball, one of the newest. It's the control of that round object which makes a winner or an also-ran, whether the sport is ping pong, bowling, tennis or golf. Sports and games use balls made in a variety of shapes, weights and materials. But none has received the intense scrutiny, nor experienced the lengthy evolution (and sometimes revolution) that has accompanied the history of the golf ball. As writer H.B. Martin so vividly described it, the golf ball is *"mankind's most fascinating sphere."* The story describing that statement is the substance of this book.

What you will read here are tales of extraordinary success and of disheartening failure; all in the race to produce the best performing ball. The narrative, is written by Larry Dennis, former editor of *"Golf Digest"* and *"Senior Golf"* magazines, a veteran in the golfing literary world. The text is accompanied by the high quality images captured by photographer Jim Coit and Udo Machat the designer of this book, making the words come to life. As a serious collector of golf memorabilia, particularly of golf balls, I found it a pleasure to encounter several previously undiscovered facts and stories absent from my own golf history bank of knowledge. It made the reading a most worthwhile adventure.

Only a rare golfer could realize that the white dimpled orb about to head out into space or toward the cup is vastly different than its predecessors. If compared, the greatest contrast would be in composition, as the first balls used in the game were made of wood. These were replaced by a leather-covered sphere stuffed with feathers. That's right, feathers. If you wonder how that was possible, you'll need to turn some pages.

After wood and feathers disappeared from the golfing scene, the ball came to more closely resemble in composition and appearance the ones that are used today. A solid ball of a rubbery substance called *gutta percha* held sway from the mid 1800s until the early 1900s. It was followed by the Haskell ball, named after its inventor, Coburn Haskell. The turn of the century adoption of this last example, which consisted of three pieces — a core, rubber windings, and a cover — was one example of a revolution in ball making. It's a tale of ingenuity, perseverance, legal challenge and intrigue which will capture your imagination. The core of the ball alone is a story in itself, having been made of everything from a solid material such as steel, wood, celluloid, and rubber to a non-solid hollow sack filled with one of the following ingredients: mercury, treacle, hair, dried blood, glycerin, soap, air, moving pellets, paste, castor oil, wine, water, and honey. The last example was an ingredient in a Walter Hagen brand ball appropriately named "Honey Boy."

Whatever the ball's composition, even from the early days, there have been only four factors which have dominated their manufacture, marketing and sale. They are: price, durability, control, and distance. One could make a case for a list of four that only named distance, distance, distance and distance, and they may not be far from the truth. Distance has always been the #1 factor in selling balls, but the other elements are important as well.

Price was one of the primary limitations on the early

growth of the game. By the time the "featherie" ball entered the scene the cost of a single ball was as much as some laborers made in several days of work. The "guttie" ball changed that. The golf ball became affordable. Then, when the early Haskells appeared, they were so limited in availability that the cost of a ball at one point was $4.75 (US) double the cost of a new driver at the time! Make that price comparison of ball versus club in today's market and you can appreciate the huge disparity. It is possible today to buy a pack of 15 new known brand balls for $9.95, or 66 cents a ball, while paying $500 for a driver with which to hit it. What a reversal!

Historically a golf ball's durability has been a fluctuating problem. The featherie presented multiple concerns. It could become sodden in wet weather producing a sensation of hitting a circle of mush. When dry and struck with an iron on the top, it could produce an immediate cloud of feathers surrounding the player. Its successor, the "guttie" was nearly indestructible. If it did receive a damaging blow it could be heated and remolded overnight. The Haskell was another story. In order to get distance, covers needed to be thin and so consequently would cut easily; centers would fracture; windings would break; but players still chose the Haskell over the gutta percha because they went farther — a lot farther. A tough "hard-to-cut" three-piece ball did not appear until the last 20 years. As you will discover in the book, the problem of durability has been solved in another fashion.

Control of the ball is a golf professional's greatest concern. While the average amateur wants the ball to go, the professional who *can* make it go, wants it to be able to stop. This is achieved with spin rate, and spin is affected by dimpling, core and cover

construction, and material. Balls must have markings of some sort on the cover in order to produce the spin to give it the desired lift. Early surface marking was done first with the emphasis on marketing and sales rather than scientifically tested performance. Otherwise, why would a company imprint a ball with "stars", or a "map of the world?" (It was done!) Today spin rates for control are a much more highly promoted item in the sale of balls.

Then there is distance. It has been and still is the penultimate consideration in ball purchase for the vast majority of golfers. If you could believe all of the advertising copy that has been printed by ball makers since 1900, you could also believe that you can drive a ball 600 yards! Each new type of ball that was adopted in the past 150 years outdistanced its predecessor significantly. Where do we go from here? That is a tough question, and one that will have to be dealt with eventually, lest golf become a cross-country game.

The collecting of golf balls is a hobby that has given me many interesting hours in my study. Maybe this book will lead you in that direction. But even if it doesn't, it may cause you to at least pause on occasion when you are about to launch a drive or sink a putt and ponder: What was it like to play with a ball from one of those other eras? I wonder!

Dr. GARY WIREN
PGA Master Professional

North Palm Beach, Florida
August, 2000

A REPLICA OF A WOODEN BALL

Well,
Look at Us Now!

TIME HAS CLOAKED THE ORIGINS OF GOLF IN MYSTERY. THE POPULAR theory is that it began in Scotland in the early 15th century, more particularly in the seaside fortress town of St. Andrews. However, there are legions of historians who would beg to differ, attempting to link every game ever played with a stick and ball to golf as we know it today. Some have taken it back to the century before Christ to a game called paganica, ostensibly played by the peasants in southern Italy with their shepherd's crooks.

But while there was a ball called a paganica, some four to seven inches in diameter, that was batted around by hand by the Romans, there is no evidence that it was ever struck by a club of any kind.

The old Celtic game of hurley or shinty might be a suspect. Robert Browning, in his thorough and brilliant work, *A History of Golf*, quotes an account of Cuchallain, one of the legendary heroes of Ulster, on how he amused himself on a journey, to wit: "The boy set out then, and he took his instruments of pleasure with him; he took his hurly of creduma and his silver ball, and he took his massive Clettini... and he began to shorten his way with them. He would give the ball a stroke of his hurley and drive it a great distance before him; and would cast his hurly at it, and would give it a second stroke that would drive it not a shorter distance than the first blow."

Chole, a game indigenous to Belgium and northern France (and still played there), bears a superficial resemblance to golf. The clubs have iron heads and the game is played with a ball made of wood. But in chole, the object is for a team to hit the ball toward a distant target, such as a barn door, while the other team tries to prevent this by hitting the ball back into difficult spots. And while we all may secretly have wanted to do that to a match-play opponent on occasion, the game is certainly not golf.

The French game of *jeu de mail*, played in England as pall-mall, was a club-and-ball game, but the clubs were mallets. Another French game, *jeu de paume*, was played with a leather ball stuffed with feathers, just like golf balls eventually would be, but the ball was struck with the palm of the hand. Besides, the Romans made balls like that centuries before. The favorite as golf's progenitor is *kolven*, a game played by the Dutch. History is misty here. It involved a large ball propelled by a *kolf*, a word that fascinates those who want to go in that direction. There are, in fact, several such striking similarities to the Dutch language and golf expressions. A hole in Holland was a *put*. The ball was placed on a *tuitje*, pronounced "toitee." The term *stuit mij* is pronounced "sty my" and means "it stops me." And there was *vooor*, a warning cry uncannily similar to golf's "fore," which has no basis as a warning in its strict English definitions.

Kolven, however, was a game played (and still is) on ice or a paved court, the ball (some accounts report it as an egg-shaped piece of iron) being struck at posts for a target. It bore no resemblance to what we know as golf but more to modern hockey. And although *kolf* and "golf" sound the same, historian Browning points out that it's because they have the same origin in the German word *kolbe,* which means "club."

Herbert Warren Wind, in his epic *The Story of American Golf,* offers this lighthearted explanation of the game's beginning: "If you follow the theories of the romantic historians, then the first golfer was a shepherd — place him on a hillside in Greece, Palestine, or Scotland, as suits your taste — who was bored with his work. He started to swing his crook at stones, just to give himself something to do, and then, purely by accident, one of the stones disappeared into a hole and a strange tingling sensation raced up and down the shepherd's spine. He tried hitting a few more stones as close to the hole as he could, and when he had mastered the shot, called over to a colleague and invited him to match his skill at the sport. They became the first twosome and had the right-of-way all over the hillside." In his autobiography, *Golf's Magnificent Challenge,* distinguished architect Robert Trent Jones ponders

Rocks, pebbles from a beach and later wooden spheres were used as objects to propel through the air — or perhaps only to roll along the ground

1400s

...

*Shepherds in southern Italy develop
the "paganica" a leather ball stuffed with
feathers, as a handball.
This it is believed is the forerunner of the featherie.*

...

*There is some evidence that St. Andrews became
the first golf course sometime
in the early 1400s.*

...

*In 1452, the first recorded sale of a golf ball
occurred in Scotland. It brought about
10 shillings, which is approximately
$6 in U.S. currency.*

...

*King James II and the Scottish Parliament
banned the playing of "futeball and golfe"
in 1457 on the grounds that it detracted
from archery practice.*

...

the origins of the first golf course. "There is evidence that St. Andrews in Scotland was the first," he says, "perhaps coming into existence in the early 1400s. Certainly it has become renowned as the home of golf, so I'll leave it at that. I happen to think the course is a masterpiece, and I have a theory on how it came about. Sailors who used to dock at the port of St. Andrews had to walk a couple of miles or so to the town. To amuse themselves on the way, they would swing a stick at a root, and the man who got there in the fewest strokes was the winner....

"Eventually they got tired of the monotony and decided to break the journey into segments. They selected natural plateaus for tees and greens, dug holes in them and played from one spot to another. Perhaps they used rabbit holes for their targets. Whatever. Their sport became a succession of holes, and the first golf course had been designed."

The late Peter Dobereiner, the acclaimed and whimsical British golf writer, advances a similar if somewhat different theory in his book, *The Glorious World of Golf,* declaring, "On the other hand, the probability is that nobody invented golf." Life on the east coast of Scotland at the beginning of the 15th century was hard, he notes, with most of the men clawing a precarious living from the sea or the land. Every arable inch was closely cultivated, and the only place to go for recreation was the strip of sand dunes bordering the beach. This became a public park (which it still is, despite the proliferation of golf courses) where the town residents took their Sunday walks, men played football, chased rabbits with their dogs and conducted the compulsory archery practice. "Absentees were fined and the money used to buy drink for the regular attendees," Dobereiner drolly notes, "a splendid example of the common sense which runs so strongly through the Scottish judicial processes."

Thus, if some St. Andrews soldier or sailor returned home with knowledge of a continental club-and-ball game, or if similar news otherwise arrived, the links was the only place to go. "Now, how should they proceed," Dobereiner conjectures. "The lie of the land would dictate their route. They would naturally follow the smooth valleys between the dunes.... But what should they aim at? On this bleak landscape, with no trees or convenient church doors to play to, the only natural landmarks which would stand out clearly would be rabbit holes. It might have been planned beforehand to use a hole as a target, but the probability is that it all happened by fortuitous accident. The peculiar nature of the links surely dictated the form of golf. It might have been an act of individual aspiration, but that theory looks, on the face of it, unlikely. A Scot might have invented golf; more probably Scotland invented golf."

In any event, golf as we know it, a game played with a club and ball whose object is to put that ball into a hole in the ground, appears at least to have come full flower in Scotland, most likely at St. Andrews, where the Old Course is history's first recorded golf course.

The exact timing is blurred. As far as historians can determine, the first official mention of golf occurred in the 1457 Act of the Scottish Parliament under King James II that decreed: "the futeball and golfe be utterly cryed downe and not to be used." Since Scotland was in a practically permanent state of war against England, the king wanted his able-bodied men practicing their archery for the good of the national defense rather than playing soccer or striving for bogeys. A similar decree had been issued

TO A GOLF BALL

Long ago when first I bought you,
You were white and fairly round,
And a little gem I thought you,
Teed upon the teeing ground.

But, alas! The months have vanished,
And, if I must speak the truth,
They have altogether banished
The resemblance to your youth.

For I've "pulled" you and I've "sliced" you,
And you've lain in banks of gorse,
And I've temptingly enticed you
From the cart-ruts on the course.

So, though quite devoid of beauty,
I would claim you as a friend
Who has nobly done his duty
From the beginning to the end.

And receive my thanks unsparing,
That you've heard with dumb assent,
The perhaps too frequent swearing
Which I've used though never meant.

J.J. Hayes
(as it appeared in British Golf Illustrated)

in 1424 that mentioned only "futeball," so we can assume that at that point golf was not well established enough to warrant the parliament's attention. But there is little doubt that by then, and perhaps even earlier in the 15th century, golf's seed had been planted and was beginning to thrive.

The first recorded sale of a golf ball was in 1452, for 10 Scottish shillings, but there is no indication of what material the ball was made. Many had been tried in those early times — ivory, iron, tightly wound flock. Balls made of hardwoods, usually beech, boxroot or boxwood, became the most common. Some were turned into egg-shaped pellets, ostensibly to improve their trajectories. In keeping with the various games that had influenced golf, the balls varied in size, some as large as five inches in diameter but most much smaller. While the increasing sophistication of clubs obviously has been instrumental in popularizing golf over the centuries, there seems little doubt that the evolution of the ball has been the critical factor in the development of the game. From wood to the featherie to the guttie to the rubber-core ball to the two-piece ball and finally to the amalgam of materials and designs that make up the endless list of balls available today — each evolvement made golf more consistent and more fun to play.

Certainly those early players on the dunes outside St. Andrews, or wherever, could not have imagined what the game and the business of the game was to become. The golf industry today does $2.3 billion in annual sales to some 25 million golfers in the U.S. Golf balls alone account for $518 million of that total. From the few featherie makers who could produce four or five a day back in the 17th century, production has grown to an estimated 20.5 million dozen last year in the U.S. alone.

There also are a few more choices than players had six centuries ago, and those choices are multiplying rapidly. In 1972, the USGA listed 16 different names and 25 variations on its first conforming ball list. By 1992 that list contained 215 primary ball names and 1,584 variations. In 1999, there were 337 primary names (or pole markings) and 1,847 variations, with more to come in the near future. There were 95 companies listed as making golf balls, 65 of them outside the U.S.

All this, probably, because rabbits make holes.

A FEATHERY, MADE BY WILLIAM GOURLAY OF MUSSELBURGH, SCOTLAND circa 1830

The Featherie Changes the Game

FOR ALMOST 300 YEARS AFTER ITS BEGINNINGS, GOLF GREW ON AN informal basis. There were no courses as we know them today; any suitable and available ground would suffice, and absent any rabbits, holes were dug in the ground with knives, diameter and depth depending on the day. The number of holes would vary with the site. Matches were played for wagers — a custom we've not managed to shake — but there were no codified rules until the middle of the 18th century, although there certainly must have been agreement in the various locales on the way the game was to be played.

Left: Mr. William Innes
Captain of the Royal Blackheath Golf Club in 1778

Right: Mr. Henry Callender
Captain General of the Royal Blackheath Golf Club, 1807

It was, during most of this period, a game for all classes, at least in Scotland. Nobility and gentry mixed with tradesmen and apprentices on the playing fields, sharing ideas and techniques about the game they had all come to love. This often resulted in curious scenarios, because the garb of golf as seen in the paintings of the time appears to have been the clothing of the day — jackets, ties, caps and trousers or plus-twos for the upper class, less formal but still bulky attire for the working class. It was a dress code that lasted well into the 20th century, although it fortunately was relaxed before most of us came along. Even Tiger Woods couldn't hit it 300 yards dressed like that.

James IV banned the sport again in 1491, but by 1502 he had negotiated a precarious peace with England and had fallen in love with the game himself. Thereafter, most Scottish kings played the game. James IV was killed in the 1513 battle of Flodden when Scotland and England again went briefly to war. But James V had his own private links in East Lothian. His daughter, Mary Queen of Scots, learned the game early and, in 1567, was castigated for playing golf shortly after the murder of her husband, Lord Darnley. And when James VI, also an avid player, ascended to the throne of England in 1603 as James I, the game came into favor there and has remained so ever since.

That 1502 peace treaty, by the way, along with the advent of gunpowder, had a curious effect on the game of golf. The men who had made the bows and arrows for archery, the primary system of war at the time, now transferred their tools and their skills at turning wood and forging iron to the manufacture of golf clubs. As Peter Dobereiner points out, "...golf's debt to archery has never been properly appreciated and acknowledged. If golf had relied on the rude agricultural implements used for *kolven* the game would surely never have achieved such popularity. By later standards, when clubmaking became a highly developed art, the early clubs may have seemed crude but at least they proved effective."

The design and manufacture of clubs almost always was reactive to changes in the golf ball, especially through the 19th century but even now. The featherie was the first to have such an influence. The featherie ball period is considered, by those who consider such things, to be from 1440 to 1848. It may have been around at that early

Top: Invoice by James Gourlay
**Bottom: Replicas of brass templates used
to cut feather ball covers**

1600–1845

. . .

In 1600, the featherie succeeds the wooden ball as the choice of golfers almost everywhere.

. . .

James Melville, a ball-maker from St. Andrews, petitioned King James in 1618 to prohibit the importation of foreign-made featheries and to grant him a monopoly on ballmaking rights. Both petitions were granted.

. . .

Circa 1650, it became fashionable to play with a Gourlay ball.

. . .

In 1800, the size of the featherie was standardized at 1.5 inches in diameter and between 26 and 30 pennyweights (16 pennyweights to the ounce). This was slightly smaller than modern balls.

. . .

Allan Robertson of St. Andrews became the first recognized golf professional in 1833. Also an accomplished maker of featheries, he churned out a record 2,456 in 1844.

. . .

Acknowledging the invention of the gutta percha ball around 1845, a new rule provided that, should a ball split in flight, a new ball could be dropped, without penalty, where the largest piece was found.

. . .

date — indeed, its construction was the same as the ball used in circa 100 B.C. to play paganica. But, perhaps because of the skill and expense required to produce it, the featherie really didn't become popular until the early 1600s. At that point, we see how seriously those folks took the game.... or the business of the game — and is it any different today? By some accounts, the featheries made by the Dutch were preferred over those made by the Scots, even in Scotland. So, in 1618, a ballmaker at St. Andrews named James Melvill petitioned King James to prohibit the importation of foreign featheries to protect Melvill "and other puir people who now for lack of calling wants maintenance." The king did just that, giving Melvill and his assigns a 21-year monopoly and declaring any balls not bearing their bench marks subject to seizure.

However, historian Robert Browning offers a detailed argument that Scotland was not importing golf balls from Holland or anywhere else and that the king sold the monopoly to Melvill. It was one of many unpopular monopolies James had dispensed to raise money for the royal treasury (those for the granting of licenses for alehouses were particularly reviled). Further, Browning

The feathers held by a top hat would, surprisingly, fit into a pouch
having a diameter of one and one half inches.
The size of a feather ball.

points out, Melvill was not a ball-maker but merely the purchaser of the monopoly. He already had an arrangement with a firm of ball-makers named William Berwick & Co., and any others who wanted to manufacture balls had to do so under his license. If this had been in the U.S. at a later time, the Justice Department would have broken Melvill into seven Baby Balls.

How important was the art of making featheries to the Scots? Or perhaps a better question would concern how difficult they were to make? In 1637, a teen-age boy was hanged in Banff for stealing golf balls.

The balls *were* exceedingly difficult to make, requiring skill and, most of all, patience. The ball-maker started with either untanned bullhide or horsehide, which was cut into lobes, anywhere from two to four, and soaked in warm alum water to make the leather pliable. Then the lobes were sewn together with a fine, curved needle, making closely spaced stitches using linen thread that had been treated with beeswax for lubrication and strength. The stitches were left loose enough so that the formed pouch could be turned inside out, putting the raised seams on the inside. About a quarter-inch slit was left so the feathers could be poked inside. The feathers were usually down from the breast of a goose, boiled to make them workable, although feathers from other birds often were mixed in. Incredibly, a top hat full of feathers would be stuffed into a pouch an inch and a half in diameter. The empty pouch sat in a "socket," a hard leather cup that the ball-maker held in his hand while he started the procedure by poking feathers through the slit with a small wooden stuffing wedge. Next he used a "brogue," an iron rod some 16 to 20 inches long that was tapered to a blunt point and affixed at the top to a wooden crosspiece that the ball-maker laid across his chest, which he used to apply pressure and tamp down the feathers.

When he could tamp no more with the brogue, and when he had determined with his calipers that the ball was up to size (standardized in 1800 by the rules-makers at St. Andrews at $1^{1}/_{2}$ inches in diameter and between 26 and 30 pennyweights, slightly smaller than today's dimensions), he forced in a few more feathers with a small, sharp awl, then stitched up the slit. As the wet leather and feathers dried, the leather shrank and the feathers expanded, making the ball tight and hard. Later

Tom Morris, above
and Allan Robertson, right

it would be treated with neatsfoot or mineral oil in an attempt to make it somewhat water-resistant, then covered with chalk or white paint to make it visible in the whin and gorse.

With this laborious process, even the most skilled artisans could turn out no more than four or five balls in a long day. And not only was the operation tedious, it often was downright deadly. The unavoidable inhaling of feathers and the repeated pressure of the brogue against the chest took its toll, often resulting in asthma or other lung trouble. Most ball-makers died young.

Nevertheless, once Melvill's monopoly had expired (and probably before, in many cases), ball making became a prestigious profession and spread throughout Scotland. By 1650, the Gourlay family of Leith and later Musselburgh had established a reputation as the finest ball-makers in the land. By the beginning of the 19th century, many families — the Forgans, Auchterlonies and Hutchisons of St. Andrews, for example — had gained fame for their generations of ball-makers. So had the Robertson family, also of St. Andrews, whose most famous progeny was Allan, recognized in the mid-1800s as golf's first teaching professional and perhaps its finest player. He also may have been the most prolific maker of featherie balls ever. Assisted by Tom Morris, who became Old Tom after Young Tom came into flower, Allan Robertson produced a prodigious 2,456 featheries in 1844. Not long thereafter, he was to play a part in the gutta percha revolution, just a few years before his untimely death at the age of 44.

The advent of the featherie changed the game in a number of ways. It was irrefutably an improvement over the earlier wooden balls. Its irregular surface gave it better flight characteristics, and a new featherie could be driven some 200 yards, on average, by a good player. In 1836, a Frenchman named Samuel Messieux, who taught French at St. Andrews University, probably aided by wind and dry ground, struck a featherie a measured 361 yards. But the ball was never totally round, and in wet weather it became soggy and heavy and was not nearly so lively. And a topped shot could result in not just a gash on the cover but the real possibility of splitting the ball wide open.

The featheries also were prohibitively expensive, costing 12 times as much as the earlier boxwood balls.

Golf became a luxury, changing the social structure of the game. The Scots, with their roots already deep into the game, somehow kept golf as a game for Everyman, but it was very different elsewhere. In England, it became very much a game for the elite, a perception that only in the last half of the 20th century began to break down.

Given that ultimate damage to the development of the game, the featherie also was responsible for further improvements. The club-makers now had a new challenge. Instead of the sturdy cudgel that was necessary to withstand impact with the wooden ball, they now had to make clubs that would propel a lighter and livelier ball higher and farther. Clubmaking evolved from a craft into an art, the single wooden play club gradually being complemented by a series of wood and iron clubs designed for special situations.

It's an art that continues to this day, on a slightly more sophisticated level. But that's another book.

A SMOOTH GUTTA PERCHA BALL, circa 1850

Golf Gets Organized

THE FEATHERIE REMAINED THE BALL OF CHOICE — INDEED, THE ONLY ball — until the middle of the 19th century, when it was supplanted by the gutta percha. In the meantime, golf began to take a new shape. Some historians consider the introduction of the guttie as the start of modern golf. Others, Robert Browning in particular, feel that the formation of "societies" in Scotland heralded the beginning of the game as we know it today. Given that this subsequently led to a set of rules, formal competitions and a standardization of the number of holes on a course, they're probably right.

In 1744, "several Gentlemen of Honour, skillful in the ancient and healthful exercise of Golf" petitioned the city of Edinburgh to provide a Silver Club for annual competition on the links of Leith. The city agreed, and although those "gentlemen" didn't form themselves into a real club for 20 years, the date of the first competition has always been considered, for historical purposes, to be the date of inception. So the Company of Gentlemen Golfers, now the Honourable Company of Edinburgh Golfers, became the first golf club in the world. With that first competition came the first set of 13 rules. The golfers at St. Andrews followed suit 10 years later with their own Silver Club competition and their own set of rules, so similar to those at Leith that they had to have been copied.

Both competitions were designed to be open to the best players throughout Great Britain and Ireland, but neither drew any other than local golfers. That was one factor in the official formation of both clubs, resulting in a competition restricted to members of both. Bear in mind that these "clubs" or "societies" had no clubhouses in the early years of their existence. Post-match meetings were conducted in private rooms of taverns, where sumptuous dining and abundant wining took precedence over the events on the course. The Edinburgh golfers, after first moving to Musselburgh, built the great course at Muirfield and moved there in 1891, where the society remains. The St. Andrews golfers, along with the Archers Club, moved into the new Union Club in 1835, just a year after William IV had conferred the title of Royal and Ancient on the club. It was an era of extravagant uniforms — jackets, usually of scarlet, with gold buttons, often embellished with velvet and silk, vests, plus-twos or plus-fours. If you were a club member, you wore them on the links and at dinner as well, drawing a fine if you didn't.

Other clubs began springing up — the Edinburgh Burgess Golfing Society in 1773, at Musselburgh in 1774, the Bruntsfield Links Golf Club and the Glasgow Club in 1787. The first club outside of Scotland was formed in 1766 at Blackheath, near London, and the first club on the European continent was founded at Pau in the southwest of France in 1856. There still was no such thing as a formalized golf course — there were five holes at Leith, 25 holes at Montrose, seven at North Berwick and Blackheath. St. Andrews and Prestwick had 12, vaguely circu-

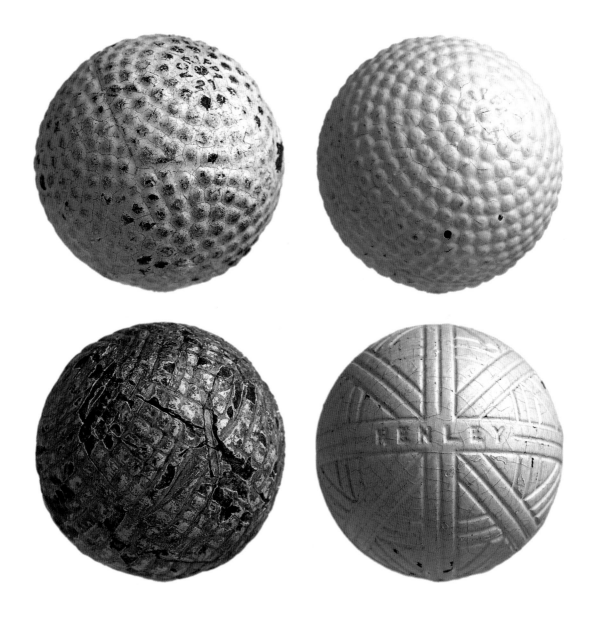

TOP ROW FROM LEFT: THE AGRIPPA 27, THE AGRIPPA 27-1/2   BOTTOM ROW FROM LEFT: THE A. PATRICK, THE HENLEY

Left to right: Mr. William St. Clair and Mr. John Taylor,
Captains of the Honourable Company of Edinburgh Golfers
in 1761 and 1807, respectively

lar at Prestwick but straight out and straight in on the narrow strip of dunes at St. Andrews, where the golfers played 11 holes out, then played the same 10 greens back in, plus the home hole, for a total of 22. By 1764 St. Andrews, because of its favorable seaside location and, no doubt, because of considerable promotional effort, had become the recognized leader of golf in the land. When the club decided that year to convert the first four holes into two, this change automatically converted those same holes into two on the inward side, thus reducing the round, quite by accident, from 22 to 18 holes. Eventually, because St. Andrews had become "the home of golf," that became the standard. And, yes, the story that we arrived at 18 holes because it took 18 swigs of whisky, at one per hole, to finish the bottle is probably apocryphal, although given the Scots of that time and their propensity for drink, one can never be sure. Although the concept of a separate fairway and green for each hole has become a staple of golf course architecture, the Old Course to this day has only 11 greens, seven of which are shared. Whether the course has 18 fairways is problematic. There is some definition to some fairways, but essentially the strip of dunesland is one gigantic fairway riddled with bunkers large and small.

Meanwhile, the game was spreading to America, however slowly. In 1729, an account of the estate of William Burnet, governor of New York and Massachusetts, revealed golf clubs and balls among his possessions, although there is no record of his ever having used them. In 1779, golf was played by Scottish officers quartered in New York during the Revolutionary War. The South Carolina Golf Club was formed in 1786, followed by the Savannah (Georgia) Golf Club some 10 years later. Golf apparently flourished at both clubs for a while but then, for some reason, died out. It wasn't until the 1880s that it was revived. By then, the game had made considerable progress. In 1834, St. Andrews had been granted the title of Royal and Ancient by William IV. The society would become the rulesmaking and governing body of the game (at least until the United States Golf Association was formed). And the era of championships had begun.

Most important, a new golf ball changed the nature of the game. There are several versions of how it came about, but the most popular one is that espoused by John Stuart Martin in his insightful and delightful book,

The Curious History of the Golf Ball. Scotland was in an economic depression in the 1840s, and little St. Andrews was especially hard-hit, to the extent that it had sold its links to a neighboring landowner, George Cheape of Strathtyrum. An outbreak of cholera also wasn't helping things. Help came in an odd form, a statue of the Hindu deity Vishnu delivered in 1843 to Dr. Robert Paterson, a faculty member at St. Andrews University. The black marble statue came packed in blackish-brown shavings that Dr. Paterson recognized as gutta percha, dried gum from the sapodilla tree in Malaysia. He kept them, heating and molding the shavings into sheets used to resole his family's footwear.

Young Rob Paterson, a divinity student at St. Andrews and an avid golfer who was frustrated because he couldn't afford to buy featherie balls, eventually noticed that the hard gum soles scarcely wore at all. Struck by genius, he heated the gum and rolled it under his palm into a reasonably spherical golf ball. When it had cooled, he painted it white and took it to the Old Course early one morning in 1845. There the ball felt and flew reasonably well but shattered after a few whacks.

Paterson persevered, rolled some more balls more careful-ly, and these lasted longer. Rob told his brother, who lived near Edinburgh, of his discovery. After Rob had graduat-ed and emigrated to America, where he founded the American Bible College in Binghamton, New York, his brother carried on. He perfected the process, as much as possible, and began producing more durable balls. And when they did break, he simply put them together again on the stove. More gutta percha was available at Scot-land's seaports in round bars about a yard long and two inches thick that could be cut into pieces that were easily rolled into balls. Paterson made up a large batch and stamped "Paterson's Composite – Patented" on them, al-though no patent existed.

It took a while, until 1848, before the gutties began showing up on the courses of England and Scotland, but their popularity blossomed thereafter. Allan Robertson, for one, saw the threat to his featherie busi-ness and quickly denounced the ball, pledging that he and his assistant, Tom Morris, would never use a guttie or play a match with anyone who did. He bought up all the balls found on the Old Course and burned them, causing a

strong stench with "the feelthy stuff." When Morris one day did play with a guttie-user, Robertson berated him so angrily that Tom quit and opened his own shop at Prestwick, where he made both featheries and gutties. The two remained unbeatable as partners on the links, but they never did business together again. Soon all ballmak-ers except Robertson were making gutties, and even he eventually capitulated, especially when he found he could make as many gutties in an hour as he made featheries all day. By the early 1860s, featheries were for collectors.

Initially, the gutta percha ball was smooth, had little lift and "dooked and shied" a lot in flight. When play-ers noticed that scarred-up balls flew better, the makers started whacking them a few times with an iron club, then began to cut in shallow grooves in a waffle pattern with the sharp end of a hammer. As we now know, surface irregularities provide lift and drag that makes the ball fly, a science that has become increasingly sophisticated over the years. Paint wouldn't stick to the smooth balls but, after some improvements, it would on the marked-up sur-face. It was applied in two thin coats, then cured for a while. White was the popular color, so the naturally dark-

FROM LEFTP: THE ECLIPSE — A COMPOSITION GUTTA PERCHA, UNMARKED GUTTA PERCHA WITH A UNIQUE PATTERN

These hand molds were used to form gutta percha balls.
The gutties had a tendency to break up, but the pieces could be used
to produce another ball. At home, at the stove.

colored guttie could be seen against the grass. But the ardent Scots also demanded red balls, so they could play in the snow.

Someone — probably Willie Dunn of Musselburgh about 1871— conceived the idea of forming the gutta percha in hemispherical molds. The manufacturing process was further refined when the surface markings were, logically enough, built into the molds, establishing the basic method that still exists today. This resulted in some interesting patterns — an imitation of the featherie's stitched seams, brambles, lattices and the like. It also was the beginning of the end for the old-line ball-makers — Old Tom Morris, John Gourley, the Forgans, the Auchterlonies, who made the finest balls in the early gutta percha days. Mechanization opened the field to large rubber companies, who gained an increasing share of the market over the last half of the 19th century. Melfort, Eureka, Henley, Clan, O.K., Thornton, Ocobo and Musselburgh were some of the factory-produced balls.

In 1876, Captain Duncan Stewart of England patented the "guttie composite," a mixture of gutta percha, ground cork and metal filings that was considered superior to the original guttie. The Eclipse, a composition guttie containing India rubber and cork, came on the market in 1885. It was effective but had a soft feel compared to other gutties, and when its makers tried to harden it, they ruined it, and it was gone by 1892.

The Silvertown Company began producing some of the hardest and best gutties in the late 1880s and 1890s. In the 1890s, the Agrippa ball covered with a bramble-like pattern of raised dots became popular and the model for many others because they were aerodynamically superior.

The gutta percha ball performed not a lot better than the best and newest featheries, although it withstood wet weather well. It did tend to become brittle and split apart in cold weather, but under the amended rules of the day a player simply dropped a new ball beside the larger piece and continued. Then he took the fragments home and remelted and remolded them. Still, it was more durable and remained round, so it made the game easier to learn and to play. But the guttie's main contribution is that it was cheap. Instead of four or five shillings for the best featheries, the gutties sold for one shilling. This, after a long hiatus, made the game affordable to the middle class and promoted a huge increase in its popularity. Golfers new and old flocked to the links. New courses were laid out. The demand for lessons, clubs and balls boomed. St. Andrews, because of the reputation of its links and because of railroad extensions, particularly fell on good times. The influx of money from tourists enabled the town to buy back its course. A transformation of the Old Course also became necessary because of the increased play. It became so crowded that the "out and in" pattern to a single green no longer worked comfortably. So the fairways were widened and the size of the seven shared greens was doubled, now with two holes cut in each.

The gutta percha period lasted for only about 60 years, but it was perhaps the most important time in the history of golf, because it was then that the game became international. The British Empire still covered much of the world, and the Brits and Scots took golf with them. The game resurfaced in the United States, first at the Oakhurst Golf Club in West Virginia in 1884, then at St. Andrews Club with John Reid and his Apple Tree Gang on a Yonkers, New York, orchard in 1888. It wouldn't be

1845–1899

• • •

In 1860, the Prestwick Club in Scotland put up a Championship Belt for an annual professional tournament that became the British Open. Willie Park won the first 36-hole event.

• • •

Professional golfer and ball-maker Willie Dunn, in 1871, became the first to make gutta percha balls in molds, improving ball flight over the smooth and hand-hammered gutties.

• • •

In 1898, the diameter of the hole was set at 4.25 inches

• • •

The A.G. Spalding Company began to sell golf equipment imported from England in 1892. In 1899, the company produced the "Vardon Flyer," the first golf ball made in the United States.

• • •

In 1895, five clubs joined together to form what would become the United States Golf Association.

• • •

long before golf would become an American game.

Once again, the development of a new ball influenced the making of clubs. No longer could the graceful, banana-shaped clubs designed for the featherie withstand the shock of impact with the harder guttie. At first club-makers tried facing the woods with leather, but that reduced the distance of the shot, which has been contrary to golfers' instincts throughout history. So they turned to new hardwoods and new shapes, gradually evolving into the rounder wood/metal clubs we have today. And it was during this period that iron clubs came more and more into favor. In 1858, Allan Robertson broke the St. Andrews course record of 80 with a 79, although history doesn't tell us whether it was with a featherie or guttie. A year later he was dead, no doubt a victim of his ball-making profession.

He missed the beginning of formal championships as we know them now. In 1860 the Prestwick Club put up a Championship Belt for an annual professional tournament, a 36-hole event won by Willie Park over seven other entrants. The next year the tournament was thrown open to amateurs, and the British Open was born. Park won three and Old Tom Morris four of the first eight. Then

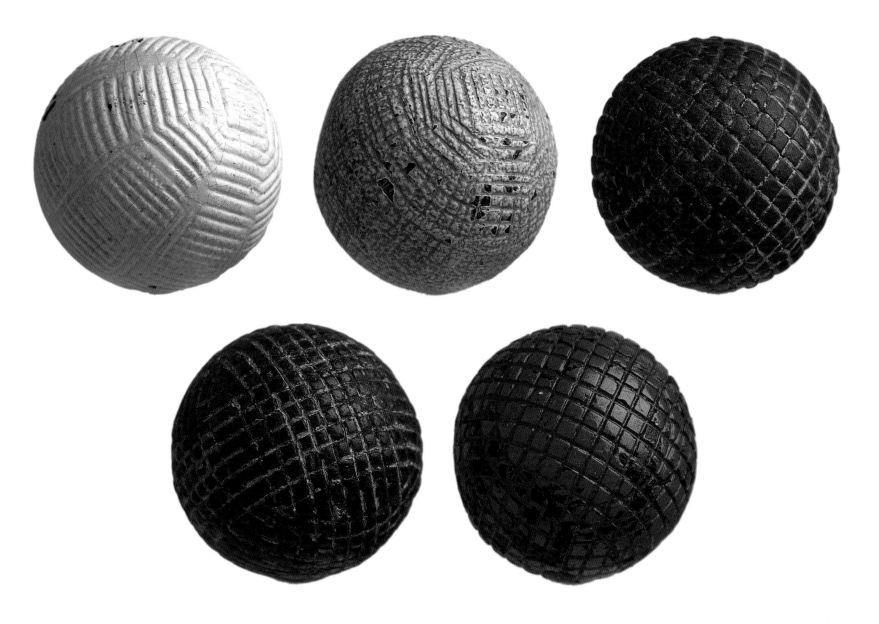

TOP ROW FROM LEFT: UNMARKED HAND-HAMMERED GUTTA PERCHA, THE SWANSON HAND-HAMMERED GUTTA PERCHA, UNMARKED KNIFE-CUT GUTTA PERCHA
BOTTOM ROW FROM LEFT: UNMARKED KNIFE-CUT GUTTA PERCHA, UNMARKED KNIFE-CUT GUTTA PERCHA

Young Tom took over, winning four in a row before his untimely death in 1875 at the age of 24, some say of a broken heart after the death of his wife in childbirth.

The first twelve Opens were played at Prestwick. In 1872 the Open began rotating among Prestwick, Musselburgh and St. Andrews. Muirfield and other fine clubs in Scotland and England joined the rota beginning in 1892, when the championship was extended to 72 holes. In the meantime, golf was expanding in America. The Royal Montreal Golf Club was formed in 1873. After the founding of the St. Andrews Club, courses began to spring up throughout the east. Shinnecock Hills on Long Island opened the first golf course to really look like a golf course, a 12-holer designed by Willie Dunn in 1891. But, spurred on by the contentious Charles Blair MacDonald, a Chicagoan who had learned his golf as a young student in St. Andrews, the Chicago Golf Club built the country's first 18-hole course in 1893. Thereafter the game spread rapidly in both the east and midwest.

MacDonald, who became equally renowned as a course architect and a thorn in everybody's side, inadvertently caused the creation of the United States Golf

Association by protesting his losses in what was to have been the first national amateur championship at Newport in 1894, then in a later "national amateur" match-play tournament at St. Andrews Golf Club in New York.

Deciding that a ruling body was needed, five clubs — Newport, Shinnecock Hills, The Country Club at Brookline, Massachusetts, St. Andrews in New York, and Chicago Golf Club — banded together in December of 1894 to form what became, after a couple of name changes, the United States Golf Association. Theodore Havemeyer was named the first president. MacDonald was named second vice president. True to his wishes, MacDonald won the first "official" U.S. Amateur at Newport the following year. The first U.S. Open was conducted at Newport the next day, almost as an afterthought. Horace Rawlins topped an 11-man field, beating Willie Dunn by two strokes with a 36-hole score of 173.

In Britain, meanwhile, the "Great Triumvirate" of J.H. Taylor, Harry Vardon and James Braid came into prominence when Taylor won the first of two consecutive British Open Championships in 1894. Vardon won in 1896 and again in '98 and '99, and for the next 20 years,

until World War I temporarily halted the championship after 1914, the three were to be the dominant players on that side of the Atlantic. And sometimes on this side.

In 1898, back in the United States, Beatrix Hoyt of Shinnecock won her third straight U.S. Women's Amateur. She was to retire two years later at the age of 20. Women were overcoming early male resistance — which remains to some extent today — shortening their skirts to just the top of the ankle and loosening their blouses so they could crack the ball farther. Hoyt could score in the 80s and Peggy Curtis, one of the sisters who bequeathed the Curtis Cup for international women's amateur play, was longer than most men. The U.S. Open was expanded to 72 holes and was held for the first time at a course separate from the Amateur. Fred Herd won it at Myopia Hunt Club in Massachusetts. Golf was on its way around the world. The Reverend Dr. Rob Paterson, who ironically never played golf again once he emigrated to the U.S., would have been proud at the progress his ball had wrought.

At the same time, there was work afoot that would obsolete the guttie.

THE ORIGINAL HASKELL BALL — THE FIRST WOUND BALL

The Bounding Billy Revolutionizes Golf

LIKE NECESSITY, FRUSTRATION IS OFTEN THE MOTHER OF INVENTION. Coburn Haskell, a young New England sportsman who had moved to Cleveland in 1892, married into wealth and become smitten by golf, apparently had been taking his lickings at the hands of his fellow players for too long. For some time he had dreamed of a ball that would fly farther than the gutties then in vogue and with which he could bring his antagonists to heel. A bicycle manufacturer, Haskell was a customer and friend of Bertram Work, president of the Goodrich Rubber Company in Akron.

It was these two social golfers who teamed up to change the face of the game. In his book, John Stuart Martin offers several scenarios on how the Haskell ball actually evolved. But the upshot is that Haskell, sometime in 1898, took a pile of rubber thread from the Goodrich factory and wound it into a ball. Bert Work then found a way to heat a slab of gutta percha and press it into a cover over the rubber core.

Actually, according to Martin, two Goodrich workmen played the key roles in the ball's inception. Emmet Junkins, the shop foreman, was really the man who hand-wound the first ball to be covered and tested, and he taught several women with nimble fingers to do the job.

But without John Gammeter, a master mechanic and genius of tool design at Goodrich, the Haskell ball may never have flown — at least, not many of them would have flown. Work asked him if he could invent a machine to wind the balls, thus replacing the tedious and time-consuming work of Junkins's female corps. Gammeter, after some time locked in his workshop, obliged, producing a Rube Goldberg-like machine about three feet high and three feet long that, in short, spun on two rubber

threads at once in the "great circle" pattern that is still used for wound balls. The threads were (and still are in three-piece wound balls) wound around a core, which has varied over the years from solid to liquid-filled, usually of rubber, depending on the brand.

The Haskell ball was greeted with both wonderment and derision. It traveled anywhere from 20 to 50 yards farther than the guttie. Mis-hit shots with the guttie went nowhere. With the Haskell they bounded along for a much greater distance. The public, both the professional and amateur variety, was enthralled. The traditionalists (yes, they existed even then), especially in Great Britain, sneered that the ball was "unsporting." They called it the Bounding Billy, which indeed it was. Nevertheless, before Gammeter had perfected his winding machine and while the ball was still in short supply, the black-market price in Great Britain soared to $7.50 per ball, compared to the set retail price of $6 a dozen.

There were some early problems. Players had trouble getting used to the ball's liveliness around and on the greens. Moreover, the first Haskell balls reacted irregularly, ducking and diving much as the first smooth gutties, even though the cover was grooved. This was reme-died quite by accident. Haskell also was a member of the Chicago Golf Club in Wheaton, Illinois, where Jim Foulis, a noted player of the time, was the professional. Gutties, of course, could be remolded, and Foulis preferred the mold of the brambled "Agrippa" pattern, with raised bumps on the ball. While remolding a batch of old gutties, Foulis accidentally included a used Haskell. When he played the ball, assuming it was just another guttie, it per-formed so dramatically well that he cut it open and dis-covered what he had done. What he had done was finish what Haskell and Work had started, which was to change the game of golf forever.

Some golf historians say the introduction of the steel shaft was golf's turning point. Others point to the later two-piece ball or the use of graphite or perimeter weighting or the metal wood. But no less than Bobby Jones once said, "Without question the most significant change in golf equipment since the inception of the game was the development of the wound ball." Courses had to be lengthened to accommodate the greater distances the ball traveled. Prior to the Haskell, par-4 holes ranged from

Before the invention of wooden tees, the player, or caddie, carried a mold to form small sand "tees."
The mold was filled with damp sand, slightly compressed and then pushed out by depressing the spring-loaded plunger.
(Two such sand tees are shown on the lower left of the photograph).

1900–1902

• • •

*By 1900, the Haskell ball, golf's first wound ball, was
on the market. Within five years it would make the
Vardon Flyer and all other gutties obsolete.*

• • •

*Harry Vardon won the 1900 U.S. Open with
the Vardon Flyer, but it was the ball's last hurrah.
Goodrich employee John Gammeter invents a winding
machine in 1900 that makes manufacturing the
wound ball easier and better and, as much as any
other innovation, revolutionized the game.*

• • •

*In 1902, the Kempshall Company received a patent
for the first two-piece ball with a rubber core and
cover, but it would be more than half a century before
that kind of ball took over the golf industry.*

• • •

*Also in 1902, Jack Jolly came up with the first
crude liquid core.*

• • •

310 to 380 yards. Now they were stretched to the 390- to 450-yard range. Some par-5s were lengthened by as much as 100 yards. The difference in distance between professionals and higher handicappers increased dramatically, causing further headaches for architects who were trying to accommodate both. There were screams that the livelier ball was ruining the game — a refrain we're still hearing a century later. Clubs were re-designed with added loft for higher shots. Clubfaces were marked and swing techniques changed to induce backspin, something that never had been considered before. The face of the game, literally, had been changed.

Curiously, perhaps the biggest loser with the advent of the Haskell ball was Harry Vardon, probably the best player in the world at the time. Vardon spent most of the year in 1900 playing exhibition matches in the United States and promoting a new super-long guttie from Spalding called the "Vardon Flyer." But the guttie's days were numbered, sales of the Vardon Flyer lagged and Harry never realized the munificent royalties he had expected. Vardon did win the U.S. Open at Chicago Golf Club that year with the Vardon Flyer. He was to win a

FROM LEFT: THE HASKELL BRAMBLE, A RE-COVERED HASKELL RUBBER CORE

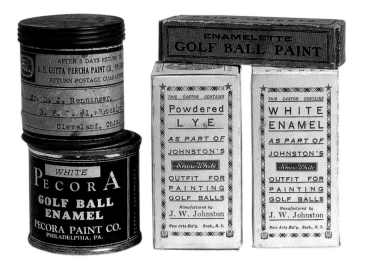

record six British Opens, but this was to be his only victory in the U.S. national championship. He was runner-up in the famous playoff with Francis Ouimet in 1913 and again to countryman Ted Ray in 1920. But many believe that once Vardon, along with everybody else, grudgingly accepted the Haskell ball, he never played as well again, especially with the putter.

The winners, as it turned out, were everybody who played the game, but it was Walter Travis who immediately took advantage of the new ball. An Australian-born American who didn't take up the game until 1896 at the age of 35, the slightly built, cigar-smoking Travis progressed rapidly enough to reach the semi-finals of the U.S. Amateur in 1898 and 1899. Travis won the Amateur in 1900. In 1901, using the Bounding Billie, he won again, and repeated once more in 1903, becoming the first player to win the U.S. Amateur three times. Travis also shocked England by winning the 1904 British Amateur with the Schenectady putter, a mallet-headed, center-shafted club that eventually was banned by the Royal and Ancient, Britain's rulesmaking body. After a distinguished amateur career, Travis eventually founded and edited the renowned *American Golfer* magazine. But the man who really popularized the Haskell ball was Alexander (Sandy) Herd, the strongest challenger to the Great Triumvirate of Vardon, Taylor and Braid for the better part of two decades. Prior to the 1902 British Open at Hoylake, according to Martin's book, *Golf Illustrated* magazine solicited opinions on the new ball from some of the leading contenders. Vardon, of course, roundly condemned it, as did Braid. Sandy Herd said, "It's a very difficult ball. It drives all right, but that is about all. As regards putting, especially on hard, bumpy greens, it is simply off altogether. I hope all the professionals play with it at Hoylake, except myself. So much for the Haskell."

And so much for Herd's veracity. As it turns out, he had played his first practice round that week with John Ball, an eight-time winner of the British Amateur and the first amateur to win the British Open back in 1890. Ball was using the new Haskell ball and doing so well that late in the round Herd asked about it. Ball gave him one, and Herd later said, "That was the end of the guttie for me."

According to whose version you choose to believe, Herd bought the last four Haskell balls in the Hoylake golf shop, or he played the entire 72 holes with a single Haskell ball, which cracked open on the final nine and had the rubber winding hanging out. In any event, he won his first and only Open with a score of 307, beating Vardon and Braid by a single stroke.

Vardon claimed that the new ball cost him the victory, producing the ultimate in rationalization. Playing in the final round with Scotland's Peter McEwen, who was playing the Haskell ball, Vardon said he watched McEwen consistently pitch short and have his ball run toward the hole. So Vardon pitched short and watched his guttie stop dead. And thank you, Harry, for that excuse. After the 1902 Open, practically everybody, including Vardon, switched to the rubber-cored ball.

The revolution had come. With an exception or two, the method of manufacturing golf balls remained essentially the same for about the next 70 years. Balata replaced gutta percha and different cores, including steel, were tried, but the principle remained the same.

THE SPALDING DOT, A RUBBER CORE GOLF BALL

The Era of Spalding and Dimples Begins

ALBERT GOODWILL SPALDING WAS PRIMARILY A BASEBALL PITCHER, not a businessman. Ironically, he helped found, and stamped his name on, one of the most successful businesses in American history. Stepping into the spotlight as a 17-year-old amateur in 1867 who beat the best team in the country, the touring National Baseball Club of Washington, D.C., Spalding eventually turned professional and went on to become one of the guiding lights in baseball's infancy. He pitched for the early Boston Red Stockings, leading them to four straight national championships.

Legend has it that he pitched 301 games during that span and won 241 of them. He helped found the National Baseball League in 1876, then joined a new team called the Chicago White Stockings, who he pitched to the National League's first championship, pitching in all of the club's 66 games and winning 52 of them. In 1939, some 24 years after his death, he was elected to the Baseball Hall of Fame. More important to the sportsmen of the world today, Al joined with his brother J. Walter in 1876 to launch a sporting goods company called A.G. Spalding and Bros. whose basic purpose was to sell baseball equipment, including a ball that Spalding himself had developed that would be the official major league baseball for the next 100 years. Their brother-in-law, Will Brown, a banker, came on board two years later and grew the business dramatically, making it the biggest sporting goods company in the country.

Julian Curtiss, a former Yale football player and oarsman who had joined the Spalding sales force several years earlier, was sent to England in 1892 to buy merchandise and investigate the production of English footballs. There he discovered golf, bought some $400 worth of clubs and shipped them back to the office at Spalding. Though greeted coolly, it turned out to be the most important investment Spalding ever made. The goods quickly sold out and were re-ordered. Curtiss had stumbled into the start of America's first golf boom.

Spalding at this point had expanded beyond baseball into other sports that were growing in popularity in the U.S., but it took the company four more years to begin listing golf products in its catalog. Spalding began making its own clubs and balls at its plant in Chicopee, Massachusetts, in 1895, but its 1896 catalog featured the Silvertown Ball, a British import to which Spalding held exclusive rights in the U.S. Its own "Spalding" ball was given second billing. By 1897, J. Walter and the other Spalding executives were convinced enough of golf's future to sign Harry Vardon to promote the Vardon Flyer and to utilize his expertise to manufacture clubs and balls. The Spalding catalogs trumpeted the virtues of the bramble-marked Flyer with lines like "The man is a marvel; the ball is second only to the man." At that same time, Coburn Haskell and friends in Akron were having something to say about that. And as the popularity of the wound ball grew by leaps and bounds, Spalding's leaders grimly decided to bite the bullet. After a futile lawsuit attempting to invalidate the Haskell patent, the company bought a Haskell license and retooled its equipment at Chicopee — not an inexpensive task.

In 1899 there occurred another overlooked but significant advancement in the game. George F. Grant of Boston invented the first golf tee. This replaced the damp sand from a sandbox that heretofore had been molded into a small pyramid on which the ball was placed. Grant's tee eventually was replaced by another wooden tee invented by William Lowell, a dentist, in 1920. Lowell's tee is essentially the one that remains in use today.

Spalding's first wound ball was the "Wizard," also carrying the popular bramble pattern and "manufactured from gutta percha and other resilient materials from a recipe known only to ourselves." Spalding had bought a Massachusetts rubber company that had found balata, a gum from the bully-tree in nearby Latin America, to be softer and more elastic than gutta percha, and balata was one of the "other materials." Soon, of course, it would totally supersede the guttie cover.

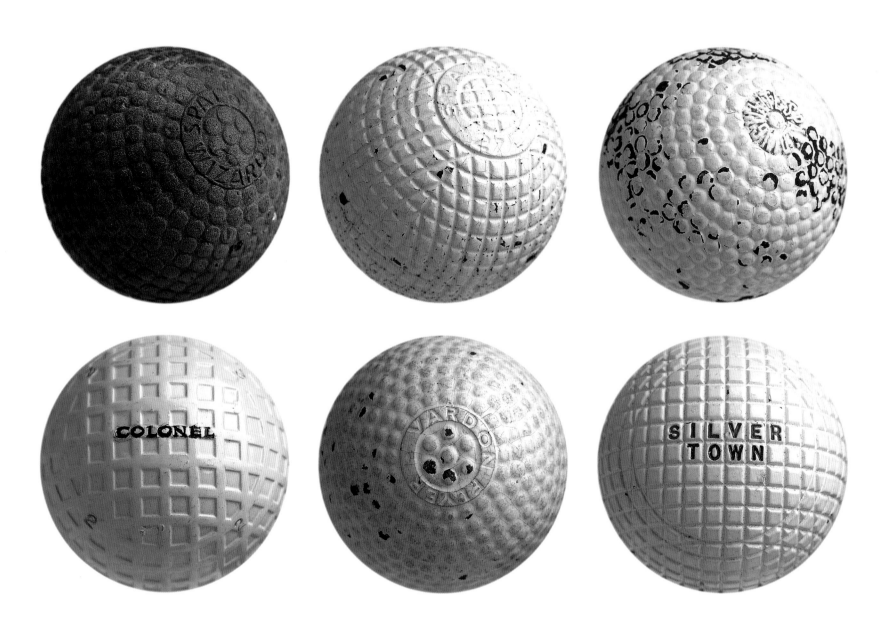

TOP ROW FROM LEFT: THE SPALDING WIZARD, THE SPALDING GUTTA PERCHA, THE WHITE SPALDING RUBBER CORE
BOTTOM ROW FROM LEFT: THE COLONEL NO. I, THE VARDON FLYER, THE SILVER TOWN GUTTA PERCHA

TOP ROW FROM LEFT: THE SPALDING DOT, THE SPALDING BRAMBLE, THE ST. MUNGO COLONEL
BOTTOM ROW FROM LEFT: THE SPALDING UNI-CORE, THE SPALDING POWER-FLITE, THE SPALDING ERA-I

Further, Spalding claimed the Wizard's core was wound tighter than other balls. so consequently it would travel farther. In its 1904 catalog, Spalding boasted that "the Wizard golf ball's durability is as great an improvement in its way as the rubber-cored ball is over the now obsolete solid gutta ball." It had redesigned the ball that year to give it more "click," but unfortunately it began to fall apart in play. The company quickly went back to its old method, at least for the time being, making a ball that "left the club like a ghost in the night." It even offered to exchange good balls for bad, another example of its astute marketing ability. Despite this temporary setback, Spalding balls were becoming favorites with the better players. In 1905, Willie Anderson won his third consecutive U.S. Open and his fourth in five years, H. Chandler Egan won the U.S. Amateur and James Braid the World Open, all with Spalding balls. By 1906 Spalding began using the name "Dot" for some of its balls, including on the original Wizard and another line of Wizards called "Whites." The Spalding Dot, in one form or another, would be around for several years and would be revived to fly again in the pre- and post-World War II years.

By now Spalding was dominant in the sporting goods field, and its willingness to ride the winds of change further entrenched it as the leader. There were some challengers, but for almost the next half century, Spalding was the primary innovator in golf ball design and virtually owned the golf business, around the world. Golf balls now were selling for $6 a dozen (you could get remakes for $4) and golf products soon accounted for more than half the company's total sales. And Julian Curtiss, the man who brought the game to Spalding's attention, became president of the company.

When it wasn't coming up with its own innovations, Spalding was quick to implement those of others. In 1906, an English engineer named William Taylor applied for a patent on dimples, described variously as "numerous ridges... enclosing isolated polygonal cavities" and "an inverted bramble pattern of isolated cavities substantially circular in plan... evenly distributed, shallow, and their sides, particularly at the lip of the cavity, must be steep."

Taylor was covering all bases. The first description resulted in the mesh pattern first produced by Silvertown and later by others. The second is essentially the dimple we know today. Taylor indicated specific depths and widths, but basically he prescribed that the dimple be shallow and suggested that the depressions occupy not less than one-quarter nor more than three-quarters of the ball's surface. The steepness of the dimples was essential to hanging flight, he said, but excessive depth would be detrimental to length. He had a prescient awareness of how dimple design affected the aerodynamic principles of lift and drag. The dimples, Taylor declared, would produce a better flight pattern — "a sustained, hanging flight giving a flat trajectory with a slight rising tendency, particularly toward the end of the flight" — than previous balls. Taylor also claimed the dimples would add tensile strength and elasticity to the cover.

The patent was granted in 1908, and the next year Spalding was the first to capitalize, introducing the Taylor-patented Dimples ball in a couple of versions — the Glory, a red, white and blue-dotted floater, and the Black & White, a slightly smaller and heavier sinker that had about 10 percent more dimples. Both were immediately popular, despite the fact that they were priced at an unheard of $9 a dozen (the same catalog offered "Vardon

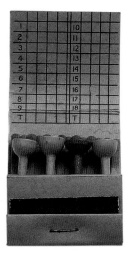

1900s

•••

Spalding balls were becoming favored by the better
players — in 1905, Willie Anderson won the U.S. Open,
H. Chandler Egan won the U.S. Amateur and
James Braid won the World Open,
all with Spalding balls.

•••

In 1906, Spalding began using the "Dot" name on
some of its balls. It was to last, intermittently,
for more than half a century.

•••

William Taylor, an English engineer,
applied for a patent on dimples in 1906.
Again, the nature of the golf ball was to be changed
forever.

•••

In 1904, George Worthington bought
the fourth Haskell rubber-core license and was
on his way to becoming a force
in the golf ball business.

•••

Flyers... the best solid gutta balls ever made... excellent for practice" for $2 a dozen). The bramble pattern remained in existence for a long time, but it clearly was on the way out and dimples were coming in.

Meanwhile, the center of the new rubber ball, the core around which the rubber thread was wound, was drawing attention. Various materials — steel, rubber, celluloid, cork and others — had been tried, but it was left up to Jack Jolley to take a big step toward modern ballmaking. Jolley, a transplant from St. Andrews and the professional at Forest Hills in Bloomfield, New Jersey, was one of the better players of his time. Eleazer Kempshall, a Bostonian who had made a fortune in the celluloid business, most especially with shoe eyelets and indestructible men's collars, was a member at Forest Hills. Kempshall decided he wanted to make a better golf ball, obtained a Work-Haskell rubber-core license (the third such in America after Spalding and Goodrich) and hired Jolly to test his experiments.

Celluloid didn't work in golf ball covers, cracking or flying apart. But Jolly thought the Bounding Billies could be improved by adding some weight, slowing them down and promoting balance with some kind of liquid in their cores. In 1902 Jolly bought a batch of baby bottle nipples, filled them with water, tied them tightly, snipped off the necks, wrapped them in rubber tape and produced the first liquid core. Crude as his core was, Jolley received a U.S. patent on it and reaped royalties for years.

In 1908, a Scot named Frank Mingay refined the process by finding a way to inject liquid — usually water or glycerine, although later a wide variety of ingredients were used, including tapioca — into a closed spherical receptacle using a needle-like nozzle. Spalding bought the rights but didn't make a ball with a liquid center until 1919, well after others had.

In 1902, about the time Jolly was producing the first liquid core, the Kempshall company was granted a patent for a two-piece ball with solid core and cover. It was 65 years before Spalding would introduce the same concept. That same year, Kempshall also applied for a patent on a solid ball made by mixing granules of rubber or leather, or both, with melted gutta percha. The company did nothing with either idea, however, and in 1910 Kempshall was bought out by its British affiliate, the St. Mungo

Golf Ball Company of Glasgow. Jolly was installed as operating vice president of the American plant. St. Mungo produced its own brand of "Colonel" balls and some 30 other brands for others. In 1915, it built a huge new plant in North Newark with a production capacity of 1,000 dozen balls a day. Allan Robertson would have been impressed, if not stupefied.

Jolly remained an innovator, especially in the area of liquid centers. He was among the first to freeze a liquid core with dry ice so it would remain solid for winding. He introduced mercury-filled cores and steel cores. He came up with the "Fast 'n Slo" Colonel that featured a ball bearing rattling around inside a hollow core, ostensibly to impart backspin or topspin on demand. Well, you can't win 'em all. The St. Mungo Company at Newark went out of business in 1932, but Jolly continued to make "Jolly Colonels" there for a while, and he traveled the country and the world as a missionary for the game until he died in 1964 at the age of 84.

And as America and the world moved through the first part of the century toward the war years, changes were in the offing.

THE SHORT-LIVED RADIO BALL

The Americans Break Through

A S AMERICAN COMPANIES BEGAN TO MOVE TO THE FOREFRONT OF golf ball manufacturing, so too did American golfers slowly begin to crack the British domination of the sport. Walter Travis led the way with his three U.S. Amateur Championships in four years — the 1901 triumph was the first major championship won with the Haskell ball. But the crowning achievement for Travis was his victory in the 1904 British Amateur, where he overcame hostility, horrendous weather and an allegedly half-witted caddie to march through the field and defeat long-hitting Ted Blackwell in the final.

Needless to say, his triumph did not sit well with the home folk. It was the start of a long series of events that would stick in the British craw. Travis's Schenectady putter, which he had borrowed from a friend just prior to the competition and which was banned in 1910 by the Royal and Ancient, remained legal in the eyes of the USGA. It was the first time that the two bodies had diverged.

Travis was succeeded as the United States' premier amateur, first by H. Chandler Egan, who won the American championship in 1904 and 1905, then by young Jerome (Jerry) Travers, who won in 1907 and 1908 and would win four amateur championships through 1913. In 1915, Travers became only the second amateur to capture the U.S. Open. The first, of course, was 20-year-old Francis Ouimet, who lived across the street from the 17th green at The Country Club in Brookline. Once a caddie at the club who would sneak out before dawn to play a few holes, Ouimet had found his first rubber-cored ball at the age of nine and played with it until he wore off the paint. In 1913, Ouimet stunned the golf world by finishing in a tie at 304 with the great Harry Vardon and Ted Ray in the Open at Brookline, then shooting 72 to dust them in the playoff. Two years earlier, at Baltusrol, 19-year-old Johnny McDermott had become the first native American to win the U.S. Open. But it was Ouimet's triumph that stirred the country's imagination.

Although the advent of World War I was to stifle the surge of interest in the game, golf was on its way in the minds of the American public. Ouimet won the U.S. Amateur in 1914, beating Jerry Travers in the final, and again as late as 1931. He became a captain at St. Andrews and is still recognized by the Ouimet Scholarship Foundation in Massachusetts. Like many players of the time, Ouimet had begun to play without the traditional jacket, the better to make a freer swing. Even Willie Anderson, the Scot who died tragically at the age of 30, five years after winning his fourth U.S. Open, shed his cumbersome outerwear during his parade of victories.

In 1916, Charles (Chick) Evans Jr. of Chicago became the first man to win the U.S. Amateur and U.S. Open in the same year, winning the latter at Minikahda in Minneapolis with a record 286. That same year a 14-year-old named Bobby Jones made his U.S. Amateur debut at Merion, reaching the quarter finals. Evans, like Ouimet

TOP ROW FROM LEFT: THE GOODRICH TOURNAMENT RUBBER CORE, THE U.S. TIGER RUBBER CORE
BOTTOM ROW FROM LEFT: THE ARMY-NAVY RUBBER CORE, THE SILVER KING RUBBER CORE, THE SCOTCH HASKELL RUBBER CORE

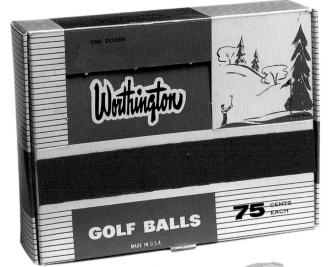

not one of the bluebloods who were predominant in the American golf society at the time, would win the Amateur again in 1920 and would remain a lifelong amateur.

Walter Hagen's victory in the 1914 U.S. Open at Midlothian in Chicago ensured a streak of six straight years with an American champion. And after the Open was suspended in 1917 and 1918 because of the war, Hagen won it again in 1919. Ray and Vardon finished one-two in 1920, but that was clearly a last hurrah for players from across the sea. When Walter Hagen became the first American-born player to win the British Open in 1922 at Royal St. George's, the revolution was complete. After Arthur Havers' victory in 1923, Americans would win the next 10 in a row. During this period, American women began flexing their competitive muscles as well. In 1910, for example, Dorothy Campbell won the U.S., British and Canadian Women's Amateur Championships.

On January 16, 1916, a luncheon was held in New York that led to the formation of the Professional Golfers Association of America. Tom McNamara, three times a runner-up in the U.S. Open and a salesman in department store magnate John Wanamaker's pro golf department, recognized the need for an organization similar to the British PGA. He suggested this to Rodman Wanamaker, the boss's son, who leaped on the idea as a way to cut down rival Spalding, which had a near monopoly in professional golf. A number of leading area professionals, including Walter Hagen, as well as several prominent amateurs, including Ouimet and A.W. Tillinghast, attended. Wanamaker offered to give the new organization cash prizes and a trophy, which is still awarded to the PGA champion.

After several more meetings, the PGA was formed, and Jim Barnes won the first championship later that summer. The PGA Championship was suspended because of the war in 1917 and 1918, as were all the USGA championships. In 1919, Barnes returned to win it again. More and better courses were being built. Although the explosion would come after the war, the period from 1903 to 1919 saw the opening of gems like Oakmont, National Golf Links, Merion East, Pine Valley and Pebble Beach, which still today rank among the best in the world. All this fueled the demand for golf balls and spawned some major rivals to Spalding, Haskell and Kempshall. One such was George

1907–1914

...

*When William Taylor's dimple patent was granted in
1908, Spalding was the first to take advantage,
introducing its "Glory" line of balls.*

...

*In 1913, the A.G. Spalding Company published its first
catalog exclusively devoted to golf products.*

...

*In 1914, the Wilson Company, a Chicago meatpacking
concern, branched out into the golf business.
It was to become a major player in the years
that followed.*

...

*The Professional Golfers Association of America was
formed in January of 1916. Jim Barnes won the first
PGA Championship later that summer.*

...

*Albert Penfold, hired by Dunlop in 1919, put his
"lattice" design on the Maxfli ball and moved
the company to the forefront of ball manufacturing.*

...

Worthington, a friend and golf companion of Coburn Haskell who, like Haskell, manufactured bicycles, tricycles, velocipedes and wheel chairs. In 1904 he bought the fourth Haskell rubber-core license, set up a small shop and began making golf balls with a bewildering variety of raised cover patterns, including the famous diamond stud within a diamond crater design (Spalding's patent prevented him from making dimples). He was an inventive genius who devised his own ball-winding machine and once, in 1910, introduced a ball whose core, he said, was enlivened with particles of radium, discovered that year by Marie Curie.

The "Radio" ball didn't last long, when it eventually proved to be not necessarily livelier at all, but it did contribute in some measure to the company's eventual success. Along the way, Worthington made not only its own balls but balls for many other companies, including the Wilson meat-packing company when it branched out into sporting goods in 1914 and, for a while the U.S. Rubber company. By 1954 the Worthington Ball Company in Ohio became the largest manufacturer of golf balls exclusively in the world. It was bought in 1966 by Victor Comptometer Corporation and moved to a modern plant

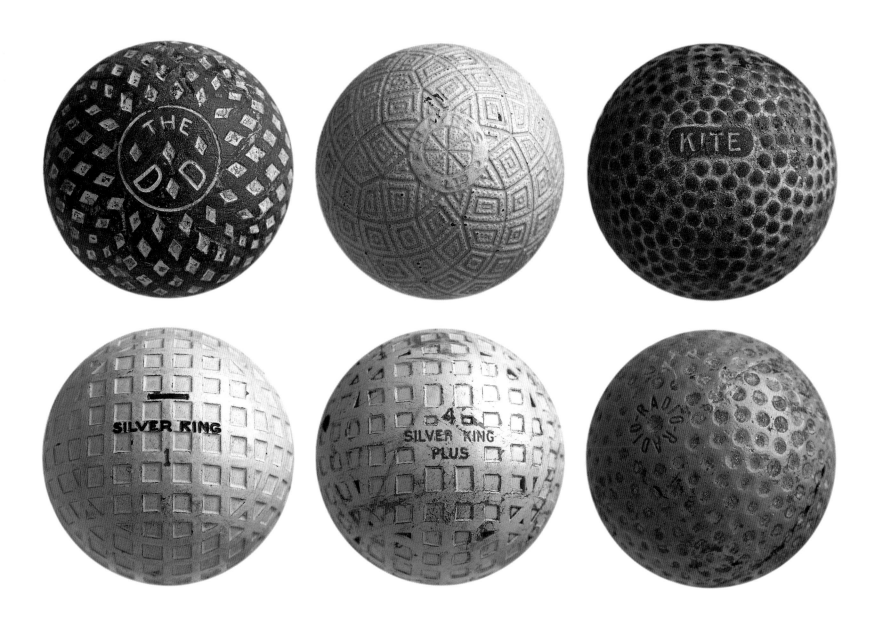

THE TOP ROW FROM LEFT: THE DD RUBBER CORE, F.H. HAYES "THE VAIL" RUBBER CORE, THE KITE RUBBER CORE
BOTTOM ROW FROM LEFT: THE SILVER KING RUBBER CORE, THE SILVER KING PLUS RUBBER CORE, THE RADIO RUBBER CORE BALL

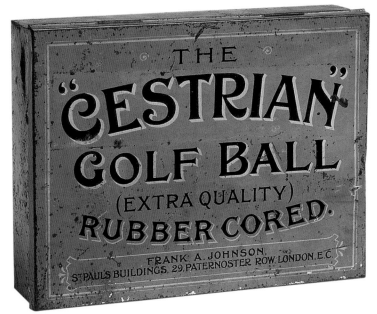

in suburban Chicago that produced 1.5 million dozen balls a year. Victor became PGA Victor, then PGA Golf, then Tommy Armour, now Teardrop Golf, and the company no longer makes golf balls.

In about 1905, the Haskell patent was invalidated in Britain (by ruling of a British judge, of course) on the basis of two earlier instances of winding rubber around a core, although neither of them by a commercial manufacturer. This opened the floodgates. Led by Hutchinson, Main & Co., which made balls called Eagle, Kite and Hawk, and spurred by Vardon's grudging acceptance, the movement to rubber-cored balls became a mad dash. Literally hundreds, most of them badly made, inundated the British market.

The only British company initially to challenge the American triumvirate was St. Mungo, eventually St. Mungo/Kempshall, but the India Rubber & Gutta Percha Company, home of the famed Silvertown guttie, soon moved into prominence. The company became British Goodrich and later British Tire & Rubber Company, and one of its young employees became instrumental in developing the British market, not to mention making an

impact in the States. Albert Edward Penfold supervised the introduction of the first Silvertown rubber-core entry, dubbed the Silver King, about 1912. The ball featured a cover of cross-hatched ridges in a mesh pattern, the areas between the ridges recessed rather than raised as they were in the old Silvertown guttie. Penfold patented both the mesh design and a "lattice" design with slightly curved longitudinal ridges. He granted the mesh patent to his employers, but he kept the lattice patent for himself.

In 1908, the Dunlop Rubber Company, which was to become one of the world's leading tire companies, began making golf balls. But it wasn't until it lured Penfold away from Silvertown in 1919 that it became a major player in the business. Penfold designed a ball that incorporated refinements in the core, thread, windings and cover, which he embossed with his own "lattice" design. He called the ball "MaxFli" and it thrust Dunlop into the ballmaking forefront. With considerable modern modification, the ball is still being made and played today (in fact, it's incorporated into the company's name, the Dunlop Maxfli Corporation, in the United States), making it the oldest ball name currently on the market.

THE U.S. NOBBY RUBBER CORE BALL

Bringing Order Out of Chaos

COBURN HASKELL'S UNITED STATES PATENT ON THE RUBBER-CORE ball expired in 1916. In anticipation of this, the United States Rubber Company, having had no previous inclination to pay royalties to Goodrich, its largest competitor, hired an analyst named Ernest Bradford to find out just how important the golf ball market was. Bradford's 1917 survey reported that there were 1,200 courses and between 250–300,000 players in the U.S. alone who bought more than a half-million dozen balls from just 10 manufacturers.

At that point, U.S. Rubber, the nation's largest producer of footwear, clothing, hoses, belting, bicycle and eventually automobile tires, immediately went into the ball business. Again not wanting to pay royalties on Goodrich's Gammeter winding machine, U.S. Rubber commissioned Harry Cobb, a member of its mechanical staff, to come up with something different. Cobb developed a machine that produced a "basket-weave" pattern that was more open than Gammeter's "great circle" pattern and one that would allow the cover to grip more firmly when molded onto the wound core. Spalding still having the exclusive patent on dimples, U.S. Rubber's first cover featured raised buttons, simulating those on its Nobby Tread tires. The U.S. Nobby, however, soon gave way to the U.S. Royal, and the company switched its rubber core to a steel pellet. The steel center produced a heavy, dead feel, however, so the company switched to a liquid center. And despite some objections to the name, it remained Royal. The company today, in fact, is called Uniroyal. It no longer makes golf balls, but some 50 years after its entry into the field, it became one of the key players in another sea-change transformation.

Meanwhile, the Royal and Ancient and the USGA were working to bring order out of chaos in the golf ball business. During the rubber-core explosion in the first 20 years of the century, the weights and sizes of ball were all over the lot, mostly on purpose. In 1913, for example, Spalding introduced its Domino family of balls with four dots at each pole — the big and heavy Black, the medium and heavy Blue, the medium and light Red, and two very small balls, the medium-weight Baby and the Midget. This was not unusual. Manufacturers were running the gamut from the small, heavy "sinkers" to the large, light "floaters." Goodyear Tire and Rubber even produced a pneumatic ball with compressed air in the core. It didn't last long, having a distressing tendency to explode.

Theoretically, you played the ball that matched your swing characteristics, a choice we are still being asked to make today. But, upset over the wildly differing playing characteristics, the R&A set about drawing up limitations. In 1920, with agreement by the USGA, it decreed that there be a standard-size ball measuring 1.62 inches in diameter and weighing 1.62 ounces. For the next few years, anyway, those were the specifications that gov-

FROM LEFT: THE SPALDING BABY DIMPLE, THE SPALDING MIDGET

erned ball manufacturing. That, however, didn't stop innovation, just as further restrictions haven't stopped it today. In 1923 the Faultless Rubber Company secured a patent on a solid ball made of zinc oxide, sulfur and glue. The ball failed to take hold, but Faultless later would be involved in the one-piece ball's return. That same year, Wilson introduced two colored balls — the "Oriole Orange" and the "Canary Yellow" — the first since the "Yellow Aster" in the 1890s. Some 50 years later, Wilson would be among the leaders in another colored-ball epidemic, equally short-lived. To avoid confusion in a foursome over the ownership of a ball, the English Silver King became, in 1924, the first ball to carry consecutive numbers, 1 to 4. In 1927, the Far East Rubber Company became the first manufacturer in Japan to make golf balls. It was joined the next year by two more firms, Seiko and Tani, using machinery bought from the North British Rubber Company in Edinburgh, whose plant the peripatetic Albert Penfold had just redesigned.

The first Great War now over, America had roared into the '20s in a mood of national euphoria. Here's how Peter Dobereiner describes it from the perspective of an

English internationalist: "America put up the shutters to the outside world, rolled back the carpet, and had a ball. This was the time when golf boomed. Many people see the game's expansion as a natural extension of the fun-loving atmosphere of jazz, flappers and a national appetite for recreation. The real reason is possibly more prosaic. Rather than being swept in on a river of bootleg booze, golf owed its expansion to economics and the growth of the motor industry. People were making money and the cheap and reliable automobile was widely available. It was a period when sportsmen became national heroes and the golf professional in his turn benefited from the trend. American players dominated the championships. America dominated the game. Golf shed the last trappings of Scottish influence and became a national game."

It was the era of Walter Hagen and Gene Sarazen, of Glenna Collett, of England's Joyce Wethered and Cecil Leitch. Most of all it was the era of Robert Tyre Jones Jr.

Wethered and Leitch dominated English women's golf during the period. Following on the heels of Alexa Stirling, Jones's childhood friend who won the last of her three straight U.S. Women's Amateurs in 1920, Collett

won five of her six titles in the '20s. Sarazen won a U.S. Open and two PGA Championships. Hagen failed to add to the two U.S. Open crowns he had stashed away the decade before, but he won four British Opens and five PGA titles, including four in a row from 1924 through 1927. And in 1929, 21-year-old Horton Smith won eight professional tournaments and had six runner-up finishes.

But Bobby Jones, an amateur for whom golf was only one of many passions, who rarely played more than three months out of the year and who would go months without touching a club, was the dominant player of the '20s. From 1920 through 1930 he was medalist or co-medalist in the U.S. Amateur six times. Starting in 1923, he won three British Opens, four U.S. Opens, five U.S. Amateurs and a British Amateur. In 1930 he won all four of them, the original Grand Slam, after which he retired from competitive golf at the age of 28. During that eight-year span he had won 13 of the 21 major championships he entered, 17 of 28 events in all. During that stretch, Hagen and Sarazen never won a major in which Jones was entered. There were no more worlds to conquer.

A practicing attorney, Jones became one of histo-ry's most eloquent writers on golf. He also overcame a wicked temper as a youth to become a consummate sportsman and gentleman. Once, after having been praised for calling a penalty on himself in a national championship, he said, "There is only one way to play the game. You might as well praise a man for not robbing a bank." In1933 Jones built Augusta National and started what is now the Masters Tournament. And, after he had finished competing, he also designed golf clubs for — who else? — Spalding.

The decade of the '20s was a busy time in the development of the game, especially in America. In 1920, the USGA created the Green Section for turfgrass research (in 1927 the U.S. Department of Agriculture announced that it had developed creeping bent, "the perfect putting green grass"). In 1922, an admission fee of $1 was charged for the first time at the U.S. Open, the USGA's Amateur Public Links championship was started and the first Walker Cup Match between amateurs from the United States and Great Britain was conducted at National Golf Links in Southampton, New York. The competition, named after George Herbert Walker, the 1920 USGA president

FROM LEFT: THE SCOTO 27-1/2 BEARING A TAG FROM COLLECTOR HARRY B. WOOD, THE FAROID WITH LIQUID FILLED CENTER, THE JOYCE INDENTED WITH SHAMROCKS

1930s

• • •

*In 1920, the USGA and the R&A agreed on a
standard-size ball measuring 1.62 inches in diameter
and weighing 1.62 ounces.*

• • •

*In the late 1920s, Dr. William Chauncy Geer
of Goodrich and Dr. Sidney Cadwell at U.S. Rubber
both were working, independently of each other,
on a process to make the balata cover
more durable. After years of litigation,
a merger resulted in the famed Cadwell-Geer cover
that was long used by virtually
all ball manufacturers.*

• • •

*In 1931, the USGA mandated the "balloon ball" with a
size of 1.68 inches and a weight of 1.55 ounces.
It was so unpopular that a year later
the weight was increased to 1.62,
where it remains today.*

• • •

*Phil Young, president of Acushnet Process Co.,
decided to make golf balls in 1932.
Joined by Fred Bommer and Carl Saunders,
their Titleist ball eventually became
the industry leader.*

• • •

who organized the competition and donated the trophy, was intended for all interested parties, but Great Britain was the only taker. The United States won, 8 to 4.

An interesting sidelight is that Robert Harris, the British captain, fell ill just before the Match began. Bernard Darwin, the legendary golf writer for *The Times* of London who had accompanied the British team to report on the event, was invited to compete in his place. Darwin defeated William Fownes, the U.S. captain and the 1910 U.S. Amateur champion, 3 and 1.

Winged Foot Golf Club in Mamaroneck, New York opened in 1923 with 36 holes designed by A.W. Tillinghast, heralding the golden age of architecture in the United States. Designers like Tillinghast, Alister Mackenzie, who opened Cypress Point in 1928, and Donald Ross, who designed Seminole in 1929, no longer tried to emulate the linksland layouts, instead building courses suited to the terrain with which they had to work. They fashioned wonderful, tightly bunkered courses that required strategy and accuracy. The quality of their work (and others, of course) was a significant factor in the rise of American golf and the expansion of the game.

In 1926, a draftsman for a railroad-car manufacturer and part-time club pro named Robert Trent Jones, a high school dropout, enrolled as a special student at Cornell University and designed his own curriculum — including chemistry, math, drawing and agronomy — that would launch him on a career in course design and construction. He would become one of history's most prolific architects and the leader in modern course design.

In 1927, United States professionals defeated Great Britain, 9^1/$_2$ to 2^1/$_2$, in the inaugural Ryder Cup Match at Worcester Country Club in Massachusetts. The British evened the series two years later on their home turf but had little luck in the competition for almost the next 60 years.

Although Arthur Knight of Schenectady, New York, was granted a patent for steel golf shafts in 1910, steel-shafted clubs were not ruled conforming by the USGA until 1924. The move probably was hastened by the dwindling supply of top-quality hickory wood. The R&A still held out until 1929 before it approved the shafts.

Strides were being made in course agronomy. G.A. Holste, a mechanic at the Indian Hill Club in the Chicago suburb of Winnetka, designed and built a gas-powered tractor with front-mounted cutting blades so the operator could see what he was doing and preserve the architect's contours. The first complete fairway irrigation system was installed at Brook Hollow Country Club in Dallas in 1925. The following year, the National Association of Greenkeepers of America was founded in Youngstown, Ohio. It was the forerunner of today's Golf Course Superintendents Association of America.

In 1929, the USGA took the U.S. Amateur to the West Coast for the first time, conducting it at Pebble Beach Golf Links. Bobby Jones was a first-round upset victim, his worst showing ever in the championship. But it may have been a blessing in disguise, because he stayed around long enough to play Cypress Point just up the coast. He was so impressed with the course that he hired Mackenzie to help him design Augusta National.

And as the decade came to a close, a couple of scientists were developing a process that would further improve the golf ball, somewhat to the dismay of the game's governing body in the United States.

THE PENFOLD LATTICE BALL

The USGA Breaks Away

THROUGH THE LAST PART OF THE DECADE OF THE 1920s, ALBERT Edward Penfold continued to be a major force in the business of making golf balls. He left Dunlop in 1927 to form Golf Ball Developments Ltd. in Birmingham, England. He overhauled the North British Rubber Company's plant near Edinburgh, Scotland in 1928 and 1929, then turned his attention back to his own company. There he produced a ball bearing his own name with the "lattice" design incorporating the longitudinal ridges that were slightly curved. The ball was a smash hit both in Britain and America.

In the United States it was sold at a 25-cent premium over other balls, even during the depression, and was the first ball to be sold exclusively through professionals.

In the meantime, another problem had to be faced. Compression, which indicated the relative hardness of balls, and as a result had a strong influence on how far they would travel, was an area of interest to all manufacturers. Here again Spalding was a leader. As compression went up because of tighter winding and thinner balata covers, balls began to cut more easily. It wasn't until the late 1920s that two chemists, working independently and unbeknownst to each other, came up with at least a partial solution.

Dr. William Chauncey Geer of Goodrich devised a method for vulcanizing the balata cover — in other words, harden it by heating it right on the ball. The process was used on a new Spalding ball called the "Kro-Flite," which the company boasted offered both great distance and maximum durability. As it turned out, the durability was fine but the distance wasn't so hot. Heat during the vulcanizing process softened and loosened the rubber-thread windings and robbed the ball of distance-producing properties. Spalding's own tightly wound Tournament ball flew considerably farther.

At U.S. Rubber, meanwhile, Dr. Sidney Cadwell, the company's research chief, was experimenting with the same process and appeared to have improved on Geer's method. Geer partially cured the cover at extremely high temperatures — 210 to 220 degrees Fahrenheit, then allowed the balls to cool and cure at room temperature for several days. A rapid accelerator in the balata compound achieved the curing. Not only did the high temperatures loosen the windings, the balata flash that formed when the halves of the ball cover were pressed together could not be reworked, nor could any badly formed balls. Balata was expensive, and this represented a considerable cost to the manufacturer. Cadwell, on the other hand, had found a way to vulcanize the cover at a lower temperature after the ball had been molded. At this point the cover stock contained only part of the ingredients needed for vulcanization. Cadwell then treated the ball with a carbon disulfide emulsion that produced an extremely tough cover... not uncuttable, but certainly more cut-resistant than the earlier balata. And the unvulcanized cover flash could be reused, resulting in great savings. After several years of arguing over which method had priority, the claims were settled by a merger that resulted in the famed Cadwell-Geer cover long used under license by virtually all manu-facturers of golf balls.

Spalding, thanks to an engineer named Harry Davis, had come up with a method for livening up Geer's Kro-Flite by molding the ball to a smaller diameter and, after vulcanization, injecting water into its core with a hypodermic needle. This swelled the ball to standard size and re-stretched the windings so they regained their resilience. Unfortunately for the hypodermic needle indus-try, cool vulcanization allowed the abandonment of this method. At the same time, it allowed the creation of the ultimate in thin-covered balls that flew a long way. One of these was the Spalding Tournament, which was renamed the Dot and became one of the most popular balls through the 1950s and into the '60s.

Dr. Geer also came up with another innovation, inventing Spalding's paintless "Top-Flite" ball. He added white pigment to balata, treated the covered ball in chem-ical solutions to harden its surface, then polished it to a

Top: Wooden ball produced during World War II, probably due to shortage of raw materials.

Bottom: Leather-covered ball made by British pilots held captive in a German prison camp during World War II. The cover is made from a flight jacket, and is stuffed with cotton.

1950–1989

...

The Ladies Professional Golf Association was established in 1950.

...

In 1952, the USGA and the R&A jointly adopted a uniform Code of Rules, with one exception: The R&A retained its minimum diameter of 1.62 inches, and the USGA kept its minimum at 1.68. After decades of debate, the stymie is finally abolished.

...

Ben Hogan won three of the four modern majors in 1953. Later that year he formed the Ben Hogan Company in Fort Worth, Texas.

...

In 1963, James Bartsch applied for a patent on a one-piece golf ball. But Spalding beat Bartsch to the market in 1967 with a solid ball and later the same ball encased in a cover.

...

The USGA imposes an Overall Distance Standard in 1976, ruling that no ball can travel more than 280 yards, plus a six-percent tolerance, when hit under USGA test conditions.

...

high luster. Spalding's John Baymiller, a legendary name in the golf equipment business, perfected the process in 1932 and put the ball on the market for a couple of years, but its cost was high, the Great Depression was about and the ball failed. The Top-Flite name, however, was to be revived and would thrive famously.

Ball manufacturers, and Spalding in particular, were now vexing the USGA with their claims, largely justified, of increased distances that golf balls were traveling. Golf courses were being outmoded or were being stretched to previously unimagined limits. To put a halt to this trend, the USGA mandated that no ball that weighed more than 1.55 ounces and measured less than 1.68 inches in diameter would be eligible for official American tournament play. It was estimated that these specifications would reduce a 250-yard shot by about six yards.

The new "balloon" ball was far from a hit. It shortened the distance and exaggerated the mistakes of the good player, and it particularly angered the British, who preferred a smaller, heavier ball in their prevalent wind and wanted to play it in American competition. So just a year later, the USGA and R&A reached a compromise. The

British established their specifications at 1.62 ounces and 1.62 inches. The USGA agreed to the 1.62 minimum weight but kept the minimum diameter at 1.68 inches. This distinction would last for more than 30 years before the R&A gradually began to yield to the larger ball. As it turned out, the two governing bodies would need to impose even more restrictions to keep the manufacturers from winding balls tighter and producing ever-increasing distance. And over the years, they did just that.

The Depression cast its pall over America, particularly slowing golf course construction and, indeed, causing hundreds of courses to go under. Private clubs were especially hard hit. The first formal survey found 5,691 courses in the U.S. in 1931, 4,448 of which were private. The club total bottomed out at 2,801 in 1956, and the overall total would not be as high for many years. Still, Shinnecock Hills, Augusta National, a remodeled Pinehurst No. 2 and Bethpage Black, perhaps the best true public course in the country, all opened during the decade of the '30s.

In 1930, the green fee at Pebble Beach for guests staying at the hotel was $1.50. A set of nine Spalding irons

designed by Bobby Jones went for $75. In 1931, the USGA banned the concave-faced wedge. At the same time, Gene Sarazen was designing his wide-flanged sand wedge, the most revolutionary piece of equipment to come along in years. He used it to help win both the U.S. and British Opens the next year with record scores of 286 and 283. Also that year, the U. S. women amateurs defeated Great Britain in the first Curtis Cup Match, 5 1/2 to 3 1/2.

Sarazen won the PGA, his sixth major championship, in 1933. Two years later, in only the second Masters at Augusta (and the first one so named), he struck perhaps the most magical shot in history, holing a 4-wood for a double-eagle 2 on the 15th in the final round. That made up a three-shot deficit to Craig Wood, and Sarazen won the 36-hole playoff the next day. He became the first player to win what would become the modern grand slam, and the double-eagle probably elevated the Masters to major status. Years later, Sarazen would say, "Probably 50 people were there watching, and I've had 100,000 over the years tell me they saw the shot."

The PGA of America had formed an early version of the professional tour in 1926. Bob Harlow, formerly manager of Walter Hagen, Joe Kirkwood and others, came aboard as the director in 1930 and served until 1935. In 1947, Harlow would start *Golf World* magazine. Fred Corcoran was hired as the PGA's tournament manager in 1936. He also was instrumental in getting the Ladies Professional Golf Association started in 1950.

In 1934, Joseph C. Dey, Jr., was appointed executive secretary of the USGA. It was a post he would hold for 34 years.

Denny Shute three-putted the last hole and lost the final match of the 1933 Ryder Cup competition, handing Great Britain/Ireland what would be its last victory for 24 years. Shute later won consecutive PGA Championships in 1936 and 1937. Three great players who later would make their marks as instructors came along in the '30s. Tommy Armour won the 1930 PGA and the 1931 British Open. The Silver Scot would win 24 times on the fledgling tour before retiring to his chair and umbrella and a life of teaching. Diminutive Paul Runyan, a short hitter but marvelous around the greens, won nine tournaments in 1933, including three straight. He would win 29 altogether, including the PGA Championship in 1934 and

 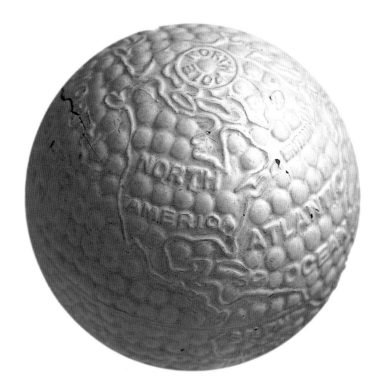

THIS RUBBER CORE BALL FEATURES THE WORLD

again in 1938, when he whipped Sam Snead, 8 and 7. It is a defeat that sticks in Snead's craw today. And Henry Cotton won the British Open in 1934 and 1937. He would win it again 11 years later, then go on to become a renowned teacher, architect and author.

Cotton's record second-round 65 in the 1934 Open at Sandwich prompted Dunlop to produce a commemorative "Maxfli 65" ball with a thinner cover, tighter windings and more distance. That same year Bridgestone Tire and Rubber Company, the largest in the Orient, opened a golf ball plant in Japan. It eventually would become Japan's major player. Five years later, Dunlop also opened a Japanese plant.

Billy Burke won the 1931 U.S. Open, the first to do so using steel shafts, although it took him two 36-hole playoffs to beat George von Elm. Just five years later, Johnny Fischer won the U.S. Amateur and became the last to capture a national championship using hickory shafts. In 1930, an 18-year-old Byron Nelson had begun converting his loose, flat hickory-shaft swing into an upright, less-handsy, more leg-driven swing that was suitable to the steel shaft. He was the first to develop the modern golf swing, and it paid off big. Nelson won the Masters in 1937, making up six strokes on Ralph Guldahl on the 12th and 13th holes of the final rounds. He won the U.S. Open in 1939 in a playoff against Craig Wood and Denny Shute after young phenomenon Sam Snead made an 8 on the final hole. Wood, who had been victimized by Sarazen's double-eagle at Augusta, was a victim again when Nelson holed a 1-iron shot to eagle the fourth hole of the playoff.

Snead had burst onto the professional scene with five victories in 1937. He added eight more in 1938 and shattered the earnings record with $19,534. He would win 81 tour events over four decades, but never a U.S. Open. He always insisted that had he not blown the '39 event, he might have won 10 of them.

"Lighthorse" Harry Cooper won nine events and the first Vardon Trophy in 1937. And Guldahl, who had retired because of frustration with his game, found it again and unretired with U.S. Open victories in 1937 and 1938, three consecutive Western Open titles from 1936 through 1938 and a Masters victory in 1939. It was in 1937 that the United States won the Ryder Cup on British soil for the first time.

Amateur golf was not without its highlights. Virginia van Wie won three straight U.S. Women's Amateur titles at the beginning of the decade. Glenna Collett Vare won her sixth amateur championship in 1935, then retired. And Babe Didrikson, then an amateur, became the first woman to play in a men's tour event at the 1938 Los Angeles Open. She missed the cut but met her future husband, George Zaharias. Lawson Little won the U.S. and British Amateur titles in 1934 and again in 1935, then turned professional.

The USGA instituted a rule limiting players to 14 clubs in an attempt to "restore shot-making skills." It also undoubtedly was a reaction to the fact that Little and some other players were carrying as many as 25.

Others new to the scene in the '30s: Bing Crosby's National Pro-Am at Rancho Santa Fe outside of San Diego in 1937; Patty Berg, who won the 1938 U.S. Women's Amateur at the age of 20 after two runner-up finishes; the Titleist Golf Division of the Acushnet Process Company, destined to become the world's leading maker of golf balls, in 1932.

AN EARLY TITLEIST BALL

Titleist Takes Over

AS THEY SAY, GREAT OAKS FROM LITTLE ACORNS GROW. IN THIS CASE, a missed putt and a bit of ego spawned one of the dominant golf ball companies in history. Phil Young, a graduate of the Massachusetts Institute of Technology, was a founder and the president of the Acushnet Process Company of New Bedford, Massachusetts. The company had started by selling deresinated rubber to other companies, then developed a line of molded rubber products of its own — hot water bottles, bathing caps, douche bags, syringes... and rubber tees. Young, it seems, was an avid golfer.

Playing golf one day in 1931, Young missed what he thought was a well-stroked putt. Exasperated, he argued that the ball was faulty, that it was out of round and its center of gravity was off. He took the ball to the office of a dentist friend, where they X-rayed it and found that Young was right. That immediately fired him up to start making balls right. Young enlisted the help of Fred William Bommer, another M.I.T. graduate and also a sports-minded specialist in rubber. Bommer at that time, in fact, was running his own plant, making golf balls for other companies. He and his superintendent, Carl Saunders, joined Young at Acushnet. They hired a rubber chemist and salesman named Stanley Szulik as their laboratory chief and went into the ball business.

For a couple of years they made only private brands. But when the Geer and Cadwell patents were merged in 1935, they implemented the technique, tightened their windings around a small solid core ($5/8$ of an inch in diameter as compared to the standard of $1 7/16$ inches) and produced a ball with greatly increased compression. Later they changed to a non-compressible liquid center, still small, that helped the ball recover its shape faster after being struck and so increased the initial velocity. The centers were frozen to ensure that they remained round during the winding process. The smaller center allowed more room for rubber thread, which Albert Penfold once called "the motor under the hood."

Young and company also came up with an exclusive thread composition and improved the Great Circle winding pattern, both of which increased the ball's spin rate and control while providing a distinctive click and feel. As a final quality assurance, each ball was fluoroscoped for perfect roundness and concentricity.

They named the ball "Titleist" and boasted that it was the best ball ever made. To quell doubters, they developed the first mechanical golf-swing machine, a double-action affair that they sent around the country. The machine could simultaneously drive two balls, either two Titleists or a Titleist and another brand to test either uniformity or superiority in distance and direction. In the meantime, Dr. Harold Edgerton at M.I.T. had developed a new stroboscopic camera to study and compare the deformation and recovery of golf balls during impact. This became another weapon in the Titleist arsenal.

1960s

• • •

1960: Distance-measuring devices are ruled illegal.

• • •

There are now an estimated 10 million golfers in the United States, using 16 million dozen golf balls a year.

• • •

James Bartsch submits a patent for a one-piece golf ball he developed by the crosslinking of thermoplastic polymers.

• • •

Faultless becomes the first Bartsch licensee, and the Japanese take out an option on his new one-piece ball.

• • •

In 1962, Jack Nicklaus won the U.S. Open in a playoff against Arnold Palmer, the first of his 18 professional major victories.

• • •

1968: Croquet-style putting is ruled illegal. Putting-green rules are liberalized to permit cleaning of the ball and the repair of ball marks.

• • •

THE GOLF BALL BOOK

In 1941, the USGA laid another limit on ballmakers by imposing an initial velocity restriction of 250 feet per second (plus a tolerance of 2 percent) at sea level and 70 degrees Fahrenheit. Plans for implementing the new regulation were put on hold until after the war, but the Titleist people immediately built a replica of the USGA's testing machine to keep the acceleration of their ball within legal bounds.

The result of this attention to technology and quality control is that Titleist began to win the hearts of golfers everywhere, pros and amateurs alike. For decades, its ability to produce consistently uniform balls through almost three dozen quality-control checkpoints has been unsurpassed, although other serious ball manufacturers are now drawing closer. In the late 1960s, Jim Butz, then president of PGA Victor Golf and a competitor in the ball business, said confidentially, "All of us can make one ball as good as a Titleist, but we can't make them as good as theirs through the dozen."

Young and Bommer and their cohorts had not exactly picked the ideal time to challenge Spalding and the other stalwarts of the ball business. The country was just coming out of the Depression, and the world was entering into war. The U.S. government, in fact, temporarily halted the manufacturing of golf equipment in 1942. For a time, making golf balls was not the issue — finding them was.

On the playing fields, Ben Hogan was beginning to make an impact. The third of the modern Great Triumvirate born in 1912 (with Byron Nelson and Sam Snead), Hogan struggled in the '30s and left the tour to remake his swing. He was successful, winning his first tournament in 1940, then the next two as well. He won six times in 1942, including the Hale America National Open, a fund-raising event that took the place of the U.S. Open during the war years. Hogan, who would win four Opens, always considered the Hale America his fifth. After returning from the service in time to play 18 events in 1945, Hogan won 13 tournaments, including the PGA, in 1946. He won seven times in 1947 and 10 times in 1948, including the U.S. Open, which started him on a streak of six in a row, and the PGA. Craig Wood eased some of his runner-up frustration in 1941 by winning the Masters and the U.S. Open. Jimmy Demaret punctuated his colorful career with three Masters victories from 1940 through 1950. Lloyd

FROM LEFT: TILEIST WOUND BALL FROM THE 60s, TITLEIST BALL

Mangrum won most of his 46 victories over that span, including the 1946 U.S. Open. Snead was a major force in the '40s, winning two PGAs, a British Open in his only start and the first of his three Masters titles.

Still, the decade belonged to Nelson. A "free bleeder" who was excused from military service, Nelson had won 17 tournaments through 1944, including a PGA (over Snead) and a Masters (beating Hogan in a playoff). He had won eight times and been named the Associated Press Athlete of the Year in 1944. In 1945, Nelson won 18 times, including 11 in a row. It still stands as perhaps the greatest athletic feat ever. His season scoring average of 68.33 has yet to be matched. Nelson won six more times in 1946, then retired to his newly purchased ranch outside Fort Worth at the age of 34. He would play only sporadically thereafter.

The USGA had canceled all its championships from 1942 through 1945. The Royal and Ancient had done so from 1940 through 1945. The Masters was halted from 1943 through 1945. No PGA Championship was played in 1943, a year in which only three tour events were played. Nelson and his pal Jug McSpaden, who also was medically

Byron Nelson

exempt from the service, toured the country playing exhibitions to raise money for the war effort.

So Nelson's heroics in 1944, against relatively weak fields, and in 1945, when most of the top players had returned from the service, breathed life back into tournament golf, lifting it once again into the mainstream of public consciousness. Hogan, Snead and the others continued the revival. So did Bobby Locke, the South African who hooked everything, including his putts. Locke hit the tour running with six victories in 1947. The next year he won the Chicago Victory National Championship by a tour record strokes.

The Women's Professional Golf Association was formed in 1944, and two years later it staged the first U.S. Women's Open, the only one ever conducted at match play. Patty Berg, by now a professional, was the winner. Babe Didrikson-Zaharias, already a legendary athlete, won the 1947 British Ladies' Open Amateur, the first American to do so. She turned professional later in the year, which would provide a big boost to the struggling women's pro tour, which would be replaced by the Ladies Professional Golf Association in 1950.

Also in 1947, the USGA simplified its version of the Rules of Golf, paring them from 61 to 21 (the R&A did not go along). That same year, the Golf Course Architects Association of America was established by a group of leading course designers. Male golfers by now were mostly out of their knickers and neckties (the cumbersome jackets had been shed back in the Jones era) and into open-necked shirts, pleated trousers and cardigans. Except for Hogan's ever-present grays and whites, apparel was getting more colorful. It would reach its kaleidoscopic zenith in the 1970s and early '80s.

Titleist took another step forward in 1948, improving curing and processing techniques to produce a stronger and more resilient thread, called Dynamite Thread, that resulted in a livelier (read longer) ball. At the 1949 U.S. Open, more competitors played Titleist than any other ball, and the company has stayed at the top ever since, both in professional and amateur tournament play and in overall share of the ball market. Even Ben Hogan, at the time under contract to MacGregor, switched to Titleist. The Titleist ascension was aided in part by some mistakes by its rivals. In the late '40s and '50s, both the

Spalding Dot and the popular Wilson Staff suffered from quality control problems. In the blink of an eye, Titleist was by them. Not even Spalding's wildly successful two-piece ball introduced in the '70s could regain the lead.

Still, more than anything, it has been Titleist's commitment to innovation and research that has kept it on top. In 1958, the company introduced a new paint process that improved quality and durability. By the late '60s it had established the best research and development department in the business and had a team in place to make ball prototypes with different dimple shapes and counts and study how this affected in-flight aerodynamics.

The '40s ended in tragedy with Hogan's near-fatal accident in February of 1949 when his car collided with a bus driving in the wrong lane. Doctors feared he would never walk again. But the '50s began on a brighter note some 11 months later when Hogan, in his first start after the accident, tied with Snead for the Los Angeles Open title, then lost in a playoff. The victory was one of 11 that year for Snead, who would go on to win the '51 PGA and the '52 and '54 Masters. But while Hogan would never fully recover from his injuries and would often walk in ter-

rible pain, the decade belonged to him. He won the Open in 1950 at Merion in a playoff with Lloyd Mangrum and George Fazio, then won the '51 Masters and U.S. Open, the latter at fearsome Oakland Hills with one of the greatest shotmaking displays ever seen. And in 1953, he entered only five tournaments and won them all, including the Masters, the U.S. Open and, in his only attempt, the British Open at brutal Carnoustie. For the latter, which still was played with the 1.62-inch ball, Titleist geared up and produced dozens of the smaller balls for Hogan's use.

Hogan lost the 1954 Masters by one stroke in a playoff with Snead, he lost a record fifth U.S. Open victory in 1955 in a heartbreaking playoff loss to unknown Jack Fleck, and he lost the Open again next year by a stroke to Cary Middlecoff. Hogan's last victory came, fittingly enough, in 1959 at the Colonial Invitational in his hometown of Fort Worth. It was his 63rd tour victory, a remarkable total in view of the fact that he never played in more than six events a year after his accident.

It was a decade of firsts. In 1951, the USGA and R&A finally agreed on a uniform set of worldwide rules

TOP: TITLEIST TOUR DISTANCE BOTTOM: THE TITLEIST ACUSHNET RED, THE TITLEIST DT

THE BALL

In my hand I hold a ball,
White and dimpled, rather small.
Oh, how bland it does appear
This harmless looking little sphere.
By its size I could not guess
The awesome strength it does possess;
But since I fell beneath its spell
I've wandered through the fires of Hell.
My life has not been quite the same
Since I chose to play this game.
It rules my mind for hours on end.
A fortune it has made me spend.
It has made me curse and cry.
I hate myself and want to die.
It promises a thing called "par"
If I can hit it straight and far.
To master such a tiny ball
Should not be very hard at all.
But my desires the ball refuses
And does exactly as it chooses.
It hooks and slices... dribbles... dies
Or disappears before my eyes.
Often it will have a whim
To hit a tree or take a swim.
With miles of grass on which to land
It finds a tiny patch of sand,
Then has me offering up my soul
If it will just drop into the hole.
It's made me whimper like a pup,
And swear that I will give it up
And take to drink to ease my sorrow.
But "The Ball" knows that I'll be back... tomorrow.

Author, unknown

(except for the ball size). The stymie was abolished, the out-of-bounds penalty was set at stroke and distance, and the center-shafted putter was legalized (it had been outlawed in Britain since shortly after Walter Travis's 1904 British Amateur victory). Some say this was the determining factor in the decision to enter the 1953 British Open by Hogan, who played with one.

Mike Souchak shot a tour-record 257 at the 1955 Texas Open that still stands. Seven men shot a then-record 60. Patty Berg shot an LPGA record 64. *Golf Digest* magazine began publishing in 1950. Francis Ouimet became the first American captain of the Royal and Ancient in 1951. George S. May's 1953 World Championship was the first televised golf tournament. Lew Worsham holed a wedge shot for an eagle two on the final hole to win. The 1954 World Championship featured golf's first $100,000 purse. The winner got $50,000, plus guaranteed exhibitions worth another $50,000. Bob Toski won it, one of his tour-leading four victories that year. The U.S. Open was televised for the first time in 1954, and the holes at Baltusrol were roped for gallery control for the first time.

In 1956, the yardage for guidance in computing

par was increased to the current levels: par-3, up to 250 yards; par-4, up to 470; par-5, 471 and over.

Dow Finsterwald won the first PGA Championship contested at stroke play in 1958. Also in 1958, the first World Amateur Team Championship was conducted, at the Old Course in St. Andrews. In 1959, a young Ohioan named Jack Nicklaus won the first of his two U.S. Amateur Championships.

The '50s saw the re-emergence of Middlecoff, who had won the 1949 U.S. Open, as a major force. Billy Casper began his Hall of Fame career in 1955 and in the next five years won 10 tournaments, including the 1959 U.S. Open. The British Open, sans most American players, was dominated by Bobby Locke and Peter Thomson. The newly formed LPGA was dominated by Patty Berg, Louise Suggs, Betsy Rawls, who won four U.S. Women's Opens between 1951 and 1960, and Babe Zaharias. She won 31 of her 41 professional victories after the organization was founded. She won the Women's Open in 1950, recovered from a 1953 cancer operation to win it again in 1954, then died from the disease two years later at the age of 45. Late in the decade a young San Diegan named Mary

Kathryn (Mickey) Wright was beginning to make her move, and Kathy Whitworth was waiting in the wings.

For all of this, the decade of the '50s is best defined by two men, one a former General of the Army, the other an ex-Coast Guard yeoman third class. Dwight David Eisenhower was elected president in 1952, built a putting green on the south lawn of the White House, turned a cottage at Augusta National into the "Little White House," and legitimized golf in the eyes of the populace. Arnold Daniel Palmer won the 1954 U.S. Amateur, turned pro and won his first tournament in 1955. By the end of 1960 he had won 20 more, including the Masters in 1958, the Masters and U.S. Open (plus six others) in 1960. The son of a Pennsylvania greenkeeper, his swashbuckling, go-for-broke style fired the imagination, spawned "Arnie's Army" and made golf a game for Everyman. Eisenhower and Palmer, who became close friends, ignited golf's explosive growth in the years that followed.

That growth fueled the revolution in golf balls and clubs that lay immediately ahead.

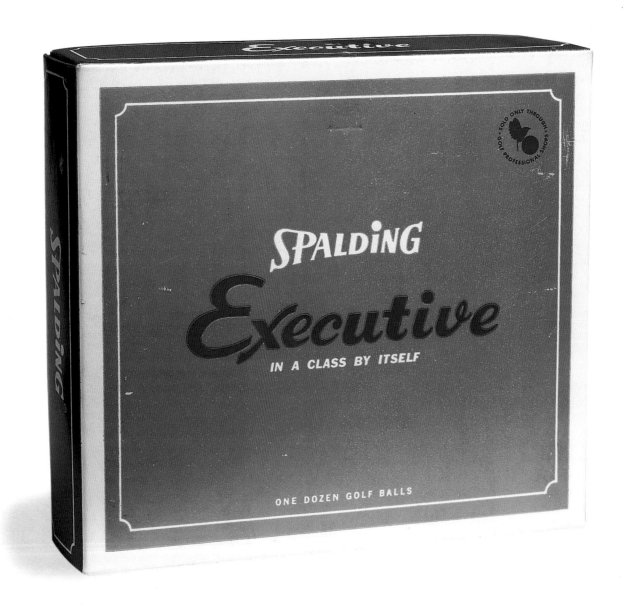

EARLY SPALDING GOLF BALL PACKAGING

The (One and) Two-Piece Revolution

THE DECADE OF THE 1960s WAS A TIME OF CHANGE, IT WAS A TIME OF heroes, one succeeding the other. Arnold Palmer was the forerunner on the men's tour, dominating the first half of the decade. He hauled the British Open back to major status with his victories in 1961 and 1962. He won the Masters every other year from 1958 through 1964. He won exactly half of his 60 tour victories from 1960 through 1964. He was the first player to win $100,000 in a season in 1963 and the first to pass $1 million in career earnings in 1968.

Arnold Daniel Palmer

With Palmer as his bellwether client, lawyer Mark McCormack began taking his newly formed International Management Group to new heights in the commercialization of golf, other sports and virtually everything else, including the Vatican and the Queen of England.

In 1962 Palmer won the Masters, the British Open and six other tournaments. But he lost the U.S. Open in a playoff at Oakmont, in his home state of Pennsylvania, to rookie Jack Nicklaus. It was a portent. Palmer wasn't finished. He won seven more times in 1963 and would be a major factor until 1973. But Nicklaus won the '63 Masters and PGA and was on his way to becoming history's greatest player. Gary Player, already the 1959 British Open winner (he would win two more in the '60s), won the '61 Masters, the '62 PGA and the '65 Open to become the third man behind Gene Sarazen and Ben Hogan to win all four majors. He joined Palmer and Nicklaus as golf's Big Three of the decade. Nicklaus would become the fourth to win the career Grand Slam in 1966 when he won his first British Open. Billy Casper, perhaps history's most overlooked great player, won 33 of his 51 career titles during the '60s, including his second U.S. Open in 1966. He won that in a playoff at Olympic after he overcame Palmer's seven-stroke lead in the final nine holes of regulation. In 1968 he became the first player to surpass $200,000 in season winnings. He won the Vardon Trophy for low scoring average five times. He also won the Masters in 1970. Julius Boros, who had won the U.S. Open in 1952, won it again in 1963, defeating Palmer and Jacky Cupit in a playoff at The Country Club. He then became the oldest man, at the age of 48, to win a major championship when he captured the 1968 PGA.

On the LPGA Tour, Mickey Wright won 68 of her 82 career victories in the '60s, 50 of them in the five-year span from 1960 through 1964. She was the leading money-winner from 1961 through 1964. In 1970, bothered by ailing feet, she retired from full-time competition at the age of 34. In 1999, the Associated Press named her Female Golfer of the Century. Right behind Wright came Kathy Whitworth. Starting in 1965, she was the leading money-winner in eight of the next nine years, on her way to a record 88 tournament wins. For many of those late '60s years she battled Carol Mann, who won 10 tournaments and the Vare Trophy for low scoring average in 1968, then won nine more in 1969 and interrupted Whitworth's streak as leading money winner with a record $49,152. Other changes: The PGA dropped its Caucasian-only clause in 1961, and Pete Brown became the first African-American to win an official tour event at the 1964 Waco Turner Open; golf became more of a public than a private game — in 1962, the annual census of U.S. courses showed for the first time more public layouts (3,567) than private (3,503); in 1965, the year after Ken Venturi overcame heat prostration to stagger through the final 36 holes on Sunday and win the U.S. Open at Congressional, the USGA changed to a four-day format for the Championship; iIt also changed the U.S. Amateur from match play to stroke play — Bob Murphy, later a successful PGA Tour player, a Senior Tour star and a golf television commentator, won the first one.

In 1968, the tour players broke away from the PGA and formed an independent Association of Professional Golfers. As a compromise, the Tournament Players Division was formed within the PGA. Joe Dey was lured from the USGA to become commissioner of what is now the PGA Tour. Also in 1968, the British PGA adopted the

American 1.68-inch ball for all its events. The Royal and Ancient kept the 1.62 ball for the British Open and its amateur tournaments.

All the while, two men who were not big names in golf were quietly working on major changes in the golf equipment industry. One was Karsten Solheim, a Norwegian immigrant who had earned an engineering degree and a job with General Electric. He also developed a consuming interest in putters, especially in how the ball reacted to mis-hit shots off the blade. This led, in the late '50s, to his development of a heel-and-toe-weighted putter that was called Ping because of the sound it made at impact. The only way Solheim could manufacture his putter was with the new (to golf) and expensive investment casting process, which he did. The putters were ugly and, necessarily, pricier than the current market rate. But they sold.

In 1967 Solheim quit GE and formed Karsten Manufacturing Corporation. More putters followed, and that same year he produced the original Karsten-1 Ping investment-cast, perimeter-weighted irons. They had a deep cavity in the back, offset hosel construction and a dull tumbled finish (by design.... Solheim felt the sun's

glitter off shiny chrome was a distraction). Again, they were expensive and ugly. But they were effective and they began to sell like gangbusters.... and the golf club industry was transformed. "Game improvement" became the in-thing, and everybody followed suit.

At the same time, James Bartsch was working to transform the golf ball industry. Bartsch, a graduate of the Massachusetts Institute of Technology with a degree in chemical engineering and an expertise in paints and coatings, had tired of his four-hour commute from his farm home in Stanton, New Jersey, to his job in a DuPont Chemical Company plant in Philadelphia. In 1959 he bought a business that remade golf balls, and before long he was in the business of making his own. They were conventional models, with rubber thread wound around liquid-filled rubber cores and covered with balata. Unable to interest the golf professionals, Bartsch went into the private-label ball business and eventually landed several major customers who bought thousands of dozens of specially branded and packaged balls.

Bartsch bought an old icehouse in Lambertville. With the help of his father, Vater Bartsch, a mechanical

TOP ROW FROM LEFT: THE BARTSCH PCR, THE BARTSCH PCR   BOTTOM ROW FROM LEFT: THE FAULTLESS BLUE FLASH, THE FAULTLESS GOLD FLASH

engineer and successful businessman in Newark, he rigged it into a plant that could satisfy the demand.

Bartsch had long been seeking a tough synthetic substitute for natural balata, which was becoming prohibitively expensive, and had been trying experimental elastomers from major petro-chemical companies. He also was looking for a new solid core for his ball that would eliminate the need to inject liquid with a hypodermic needle. When one company, Phillips, sent him a new material it called "cispolybutadiene", Bartsch, as he always did with new stuff, put it into his cover molds and produced a full-size ball instead of a small core. Upon testing it, he discovered that not only would it make a hot core, it might, with some tinkering, also make a hot one-piece ball.

With the aid of a newly hired production manager named Chet Lee, Bartsch set out to modify the cispolybutadiene molecule, a very rubbery material, into a substance suitable for golf balls. It was a daunting task, but he discovered that if he treated it with a new chemical called methacrylate, he produced a material that had the proper resilience, strength and feel required in a golf ball.

After lengthy and laborious testing to get the properties just right, Bartsch and Lee came out in the fall of 1962 with a solid ball that they felt met all the requirements of durability and playability. It conformed to the USGA's initial velocity regulation. It was uncuttable, even with an axe. It was impervious to internal damage or deterioration. Because it was so hard, it wasted much less energy at impact than the wound ball. It also spun a great deal less, which drew criticism from Arnold Palmer that the ball did not "hang" enough on long, high shots. But this lack of spin also reduced hooking and slicing, so Bartsch figured this was a wash. The ball was easier and quicker to make, cutting production time before painting and packaging from three days to two hours, and because of its immunity to heat, it could take a paint that would dry in 30 seconds as opposed to 24 hours.

Obviously, the economics were appealing. Bartsch could make the solid ball for $2 a dozen, compared to $4.25 a dozen for a top rubber-core ball. Now, what to do with it? Bartsch applied for patents and, over the next two years, offered licenses to a number of companies, including Faultless, which had unsuccessfully pioneered the solid ball some 40 years before. For a while, he had no takers. The ball was an unknown, existing ball companies didn't want to make their current products obsolete and, besides, those patents had not yet been granted.

Just as Bartsch was about to sell a license to Carlisle Rubber Company, another solid ball appeared on the market. It was inferior to the Bartsch ball but cheaper, so it was a hit with hackers and driving ranges. Carlisle, of course, backed off, and an exasperated Bartsch put his plant up for sale in the spring of 1965. There was a flurry of interest from both large and small companies, who were mostly interested in Bartsch's chemical secrets. While this was going on, Bill Miller of Faultless decided it was time to go with a solid ball, and Bartsch had the best one available. The company signed a long-term license, and Bartsch was finally in business.

Ever the innovator, Bartsch even solved the serious problem occasioned by a shortage of golf ball molds at the time. Only one company, Atti of Union City, New Jersey, made molds for the entire ball industry, and because of increasing demand it was seriously back-ordered. No problem for Jim Bartsch. He simply set up a little mold foundry of his own that could supply Faultless

and everybody else who wanted to make his ball.

Bartsch had hired Princeton Chemical Research, a technical company that specialized in polymer (chemical compounds and mixtures) research, to confirm his invention. In 1966, as the patents began to come in from Canada, Great Britain and eventually the United States (the latter was dated April 11, 1967, 68 years to the day after the Haskell rubber-core patent was granted), he sold his patent rights to PCR. Interest in the ball was growing overseas, and PCR, with Faultless and its customers leading the way, was after ten percent of the U.S. market.

Bartsch's ship now having come in, he sold the Stanton home and moved his family and the mold factory to Nantucket, there ostensibly to take advantage of the leisure time his new-found riches had brought.

Unfortunately, it didn't work out that way for PCR, Faultless and the others who were banking on the success of Bartsch's solid ball. To make a very long story short, the ball was never much of a commercial success. It lacked distance, was brittle and prone to chipping and cracking, and it felt like a rock. PCR managed to get a small share of the market for a while by getting into the

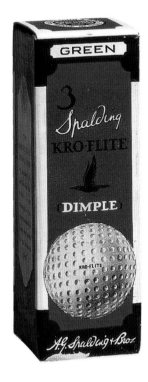

private label business, but the company lacked the money and the name to properly promote the ball to the public.

The Plymouth Division of Shakespeare, one of the PCR licensees, produced three balls — the Black Watch, the Chemold and the Fireball. Faultless first produced the White Streak, but it had the same problems as the PCR/Bartsch ball. Dunlop experimented with the ball. PGA Victor, a division of Victor Comptometer, made it primarily as a range ball. In trying to increase the compression, PGA Victor encountered the same problem — the ball became prone to chipping and cracking. After some tinkering with the formula, Faultless came out in 1967 with a Blue Flash and a Gold Flash that did modestly well in the market. But they were still too rocklike to suit most golfers. And at the same time, there was a confluence of circumstances that doomed the solid ball.

Spalding actually had beaten the Bartsch ball to the market with a solid ball of its own called the Unicore. But realizing that it had the same penchant for chipping and lack of feel, Spalding's engineers took a further step and enclosed a solid core similar to Bartsch's with a cover of polyurethane plastic. They named it the Executive, and it was so far superior to the solid ball that Faultless and PCR started making their own two-piece balls.

Despite the demise of the one-piece ball, Jim Bartsch has to be given his place in history. Without his research, we may never have had a two-piece ball. Spalding's addition of a cover also was a stroke of genius. But the revolution was not quite complete.

Dr. Richard Rees, a scientist for DuPont, had found a way to crosslink two different chemicals or polymers with the addition of sodium salt to produce a modified thermoplastic resin. DuPont eventually would call it Surlyn, and while it was not originally intended for golf balls, it changed that industry forever, thanks mainly to the efforts of a young chemical engineer named Terry Pocklington.

At the time in the early '60s that DuPont was trying to sell its new stuff to clients, Pocklington worked for Campbell Ball Company, a small Canadian ball manufacturer. He was intrigued by the toughness of the product and envisioned it as a cover substitute for balata. His employers at the time begged off the idea, but Pocklington shortly left and joined Sportsman Golf Company in sub-

urban Chicago, which would soon become Ram Golf. His new employers liked the idea. Pocklington worked with DuPont engineers to correct a few problems with the substance — it was too sticky, required extremely high temperatures to be workable and rejected paint adherence. That solved, Pocklington applied it as a cover on a three-piece wound ball and put it on the market in 1968 as the 3-D. Since DuPont had yet to name the material, Ram dubbed it Ramlon, but Surlyn soon became official.

The 3-D was a better performer than the solid Bartsch ball, but it still was a rock. The Surlyn cover was .09 of an inch thick, compared to .03 for the balata cover, and this considerably reduced its distance off the tee and performance around the greens. But it was uncuttable, and this appealed to a portion of the economy-minded golf populace, so it did capture a share of the market. Ram was able to make even more inroads with the 3-D's successor, the Golden Ram.

Spalding again was lurking in the wings, however. Plymouth, First Flight and U.S. Royal had joined Ram in putting Surlyn covers on wound rubber cores. But in 1971, Spalding came out with a solid core covered with

FROM LEFT: THE MOLITOR BY SPALDING, THE GOLDEN RAM

Surlyn. The company called the ball Top-Flite, and the ball business had been revolutionized. The engineer behind the Top-Flite was Robert Molitor, who blended two forms of Surlyn — zinc and sodium — to make a softer cover that produced more distance and still was the most durable ball on the market. Even the Top-Flite was affectionately dubbed the Rock-Flite, and compared to the advanced two-piece balls of the '90s, it was. But it sold, and it catapulted Spalding back into a position to challenge Titleist's leadership. Spalding (the ball division is now called Top-Flite) no longer even makes three-piece wound balls.

Spalding claimed that the new Top-Flite was the longest ball in combined driver/5-iron distance. In fact, that early ball was longer than others off the more lofted iron clubs, because of its inherent low spin velocity, but not necessarily off the driver, although it did have a boring flight and a lot of run on firm fairways. Its performance around the green obviously could not match a balata wound ball.

This combination of durability, distance and less spin obviously was aimed at the masses, and Spalding made no bones about it. However, it spent the next 30

Clockwise from top left:
G.C. Vare, Babe Zaharias-Didrikson,
Jack Nicklaus and Ben Hogan

1970s

...

Spalding introduces a new Top-Flite. A two-piece ball with a Surlyn cover that revolutionizes the industry and sets the stage for the two-piece ball.

...

United States Royal is the first company to deviate from the standard Atti dimple design pattern, with the Plus 6, which has 252 dimples.

...

The USGA starts to list balls that conform to their standards, with 16 different names and 25 variations of ball types.

...

The Polara Ball is sold on the market by PGA Victor, despite its being deemed non-conforming by the USGA.

...

years tweaking the two-piece ball and its cover to make it more appealing to the Tour professional. As the 20th century came to a close, it had succeeded to some extent.

Actually, the Golden Ram was the first Surlyn-covered ball to win a professional tournament when it was played by Tom Shaw to win the 1971 Bing Crosby National Pro-Am. Undoubtedly the ball had been improved by then. Lee Trevino was the first to win with a two-piece Surlyn ball, the Faultless Omega, at the 1974 World Series of Golf. He was under contract to Faultless at the time, but the company quit making balls in 1974, and Trevino signed with Spalding. He then switched to Titleist balatas for a while, but returned to Spalding. On both the regular and Senior Tours, Trevino has been a winner with every ball he used.

Throughout the '70s there was a rush to follow the Golden Ram and Top-Flite. Dunlop, Hogan and Wilson all offered wound balls with Surlyn covers. Titleist introduced its first Surlyn cover in 1974 on the DT, also a wound ball. It would not make a two-piece ball until 1981, when it introduced the Pinnacle, a name that had been on its third-line ball back in the '50s. It immediately became a top seller. But it wasn't until 1991 that the Titleist HVC became the first two-piece ball to carry the distinctive Titleist script logo. By 1977, Spalding had come out with the Molitor, named after its designer. It was marketed as a premium ball, priced at $2 at a time when other top-grade balls sold for $1.25. This was Spalding's first effort to approach the balata-like qualities of Titleist and others. The Molitor had a softer Surlyn cover that was labeled "cut-resistant" rather than "cut-proof."

Of little note in the early 1970s, and indeed not really appreciated today, was the development of a synthetic balata material, a petroleum derivative that is a rubber-related elastomer. Balata tended to vary in quality, and it also was too expensive. Synthetic balata was essentially the same product but cheaper and more uniform. It was largely ignored in the United States until about 1980, when Titleist and others began to mix it into their balata formulae. Today the covers are still called balata, but they are all synthetic.

In the meantime, the next evolution involved how those covers were designed, just as it had some 60 years before.

THE UNIROYAL PLUS SIX, STARTED THE DIMPLE RACE IN 1971

CHAPTER ELEVEN

The Dimple Race Begins

FOR MORE THAN 60 YEARS, WITH A FEW EXCEPTIONS, GOLF BALLS HAD looked the same on the outside, with 336 round Taylor dimples stamped into the cover. Until 1971, the only dimple pattern available was the "Atti pattern," simply because the only moldmaker in the United States (there was another in West Germany) was Ralph Atti, owner of a tool-and-die shop in Union, New Jersey. It was an octahedron pattern, laid out in eight equilateral triangles. There were, as usual, 336 dimples that covered 66 percent of the surface.

About 1950, U.S. Rubber had come out with a mesh marking that featured inverted four-sided pyramid-shaped recessions. Named the Royal Special, it never caught on. The common perception is that the same company, now called Uniroyal, started the modern dimple revolution in 1971 with its Royal Plus Six, featuring 252 randomly spaced, hexagon-shaped dimples (the name came from the company's claim that the ball would carry six yards farther than any other ball off the tee... for whom and what caliber of player that would happen was not specified). More on the Plus Six later.

Actually, Titleist was the first company out with a different dimple, although it was quite by accident. Somewhere in the mid-'60s, Titleist received a batch of molds from Atti that, its quality control department discovered, had dimples shaped differently than standard. They were more saucer-shaped, shallower and 2/1000th of an inch larger in diameter. Titleist made up some test balls, liked the results and asked Atti to make more of the same molds. He was not told why, else the entire industry would have known what was up. Eventually, those molds produced the K2A Titleist that became one of history's most popular balls, both on Tour and with the public.

Meanwhile, the Royal Plus Six was having problems. Uniroyal claimed that its new dimple pattern created more lift than the heretofore conventional dimples and dimple pattern. It undoubtedly did. The ball flew higher and farther downwind. The problem was that the additional lift caused the ball to upshoot and sail against the wind or in crosswinds. This was okay for the poorer players who had trouble getting the ball in the air in the first place, but it was a definite turnoff for the middle- and low-handicappers... and especially the professionals.

As a result, despite some early success, the Plus Six never found a market niche. Nor, as it turned out, did Uniroyal, which was out of the ball business by the end of the decade. What the Plus Six *did* do was awaken the industry to dimple science and the affect of different patterns on the ball's flight. And it was Titleist, as you might expect, that was the first to make an impact. Dr. John Jepson, by then the company's director of research and development, was charged with producing a ball that would go farther than the K2A. What he produced, and put on the market in 1973, was a ball that had 324

CHAPTER ONE

THE TITLEIST PRO TRAJECTORY, TOP-FLITE XL, THE MAXFLI XLT-15

dimples that were larger by 15 percent and shallower by 10 percent than standard, that covered more of the ball's surface and that were arranged in an "icosahedron" pattern, that divided the surface into 20 triangular sections. The larger dimples were closer together, so the spaces between them were thinner, more sharply edged and less variable in thickness, which presented a more uniform, rougher surface.

"We were not just looking for added distance, although the ball carried an average of five to 10 yards farther with a driver," Jepson says. "We also wanted to see if we could design dimples that would produce less left and right deviation in flight. You do this by reducing the drag force, the resistance to forward motion exerted on the ball by the air it is passing through."

The ball was dubbed the "big dimple" Titleist, and with its advent the company stopped making the popular K2A. The golf world, for the most part, was aghast at a move that was at once bold and possibly foolish. The new Titleist was indeed longer. In 1976, in answer to the greater distances balls were traveling and after considerable testing, the USGA established an Overall Distance Standard. The ODS dictated that a conforming ball cannot travel — including carry and roll — more than 280 yards, plus a six percent tolerance, which takes the number to 296 yards. This distance was determined under specific USGA test conditions that took into account clubhead speed on its Iron Byron swing machine and the turf conditions on its outdoor range at Far Hills, New Jersey. (The same test is now done indoors with computers and high-speed photography.) In fairness to manufacturers, the USGA selected the longest ball on the market at the time and based its new standard on the distance it traveled. Although it was never announced by the USGA, that ball was the big dimple Titleist.

Its one flaw was that it flew too high and had a tendency to upshoot off the higher-lofted irons. Bruce Crampton, a low-ball hitter who was enjoying the best years of his career at the time, loved the ball. But many Tour players did not, and they were defecting.

Alarmed by this, Bill Bommer, Fred's son and then president of Titleist, called Jepson into his office and told him he had six months to a year to come up with a ball that went as far as the big dimple ball but no higher than the K2A. The result was the Pro-Trajectory, which hit the market in 1975, and later the Low-Trajectory (the big dimple ball became the

High-Trajectory). It was all a matter of altering the size and shape of the dimples. The race was on for real.

Jepson also had been charged with finding a technique that would allow Titleist to make its own molds and become independent of Atti. More important, to conduct aerodynamic tests in secret, the company had to be able to produce molds with new dimple patterns and sizes!

These tests were conducted by Titleist in the mid-'70s in an old Goodyear air dock. This was a shell built to manufacture dirigibles — it was 100 yards wide at the base, 300 yards long and 160 feet high, free of obstructions except for some buildings Goodyear had erected, and with a catwalk some 60 or 70 feet above ground level. The shell effectively eliminated wind and temperature variances. Using a specially designed air cannon that would impart different initial and spin velocities and high-speed cameras spaced along the catwalk, Titleist's researchers could fire a ball into a huge pile of sand at the opposite end of the building and make various measurements along the way.

"It was a large undertaking, and it caused us to make slight modifications to a constant in our equations, bringing our computer results and measured results very much into synch," says Jepson. "It was probably the crowning achievement of our program. From that time on, we were able with confidence to design a certain type of dimple pattern on a golf ball to achieve a variety of results in distance and trajectory."

Others were seeking the same variety. In 1976, Wilson came out with a new Pro-Staff that had 300 flat-bottomed, "truncated cone" dimples that ostensibly produced more carry and a steeper angle of descent. Spalding produced a mate to its Top-Flite in 1979, the Top-Flite XL that was designed (with 330 wider, shallower dimples) to have the higher flight that the original lacked. That same year Dunlop introduced the Max-Fli XLT-15, a three-piece ball with a synthetic balata cover and smaller, deeper dimples for lower trajectory, and the Silver Max-Fli, a two-piece, Surlyn-covered model with wider, shallower dimples that produced a higher flight. It was a portent.

In 1977, a ball that straightened hooks and slices came on the market. Invented by Dan Nepela and Dr. Fred Holmstrom, a pair of California scientists, the Polara had a six-row band of standard dimples around the equator and shallower dimples over the rest of the ball. One ver-

TOP ROW FROM LEFT: THE FLYING LADY, THE LADY SENATOR   BOTTOM ROW FROM LEFT: LOPEZ DM2, THE GOLDEN GIRL

sion of the ball reduced curvature by 50 percent, another version by 75 percent, the inventors claimed. Manufactured for Nepela and Holmstrom by PGA Victor, the Polara was a wound ball with a Surlyn cover that appeared to work on a gyroscopic principle, although the inventors would not say that. Rather than simply reducing curvature, the ball appeared to make a definite in-flight correction. It also was considerably shorter than competitive balls. In any event, the USGA looked askance and refused to put the ball on its approved list, even though it conformed to all the existing specifications. A new rule requiring that a ball be aerodynamically symmetrical was proposed, but it wasn't put into effect until 1980.

In the meantime, the Polara was put on the market and sold reasonably well, even at $20 a dozen compared to $16 to $17.50 that other balls were commanding. But the USGA's refusal to rule it conforming began to hurt sales, and late in 1978 Nepela and Holmstrom filed a multi-million dollar lawsuit against the USGA and the Golf Ball Manufacturers Association, claiming the two organizations had conspired to keep the Polara balls off the market and stifle sales. After several decisions (one of which awarded Polara $5 million), appeals and reversals, an out-of-court settlement was reached in 1984. The USGA paid Polara $1,375,000, and the ball disappeared.

Early in the '70s, another battle had been won (or lost, depending on whose viewpoint you took). The USGA and the Royal and Ancient had for some time been discussing the disparity in ball size between the two organizations and were about to agree on a compromise ball, 1.66 inches in diameter with the 1.62-ounce weight restriction still applying. The ball manufacturers, naturally, were in an uproar. Now everybody would have to retool, an expensive process, and with only two moldmakers in the world, the wait for new molds would be lengthy. A group of PGA Tour players jumped into the fray, signing a statement that they would play only the 1.68 ball.

The tide may have turned at the 1972 PGA Championship at Oakland Hills when several manufacturing executives had an impromptu discussion with Lynford Lardner, Jr., the new president of the USGA. Lardner was a businessman who sat on several boards, and the manufacturers tried to convince him of the economic folly of making a considerable expenditure without the prospect of any financial gain. At one point Lardner asked why the compromise had been suggested. One of the executives answered, "So six guys in New York and six guys in St. Andrews can sit back, drink their scotch and water, puff on their cigars and say the golf world at last has one set of rules." Shortly thereafter a seven-year testing program was suggested, a ploy that allowed the USGA to withdraw gracefully from the hassle, and the issue never surfaced again. In 1974, the R&A made the larger American ball mandatory in the British Open, and in 1990 the small ball was ruled non-conforming and disappeared.

Two significant equipment innovations marked the '70s. The Shakespeare Company introduced the graphite shaft in 1970. It was designed by Frank Thomas, the company's chief design engineer, who four years later became technical director for the USGA. It would be several years before the material and the manufacturing process would be refined to produce consistent, quality shafts.

In 1978, Gary Adams discovered the metal wood. A former salesman for PGA Victor, he had joined the Wittek Company, a large supplier of sundries to golf courses and ranges, as vice president of sales and marketing. He became intrigued with the company's line of metal driving-range clubs. He began working with Phil Skrovonsky, a premier moldmaker who had previously produced an odd-shaped set of metal woods, to design a metal wood that looked like a golf club. They did, but Wittek wasn't interested, so Adams formed his own company. He named it TaylorMade, introduced the club to the men's and women's tours in 1979, and the sound and feel of golf were changed forever.

A not-so-significant innovation occurred in 1979 when Lynx, heretofore only an innovative club company, introduced a pair of oversized balls. One measured 1.74 inches in diameter, the other 1.80. Both were overweight and non-conforming, but they were never intended to be played in the U.S. Open. The balls were the brainchild of former PGA champion Jerry Barber, whose premise was that because the ball's center of gravity was higher off the ground than normal, it was easier to get in the air, especially for beginners, seniors and women. But good players shunned the ball, and it never caught on with the players for whom it was intended.

The dimple competition and the attendant off-

course foofaraw could not overshadow what turned out to be one of history's most exciting periods on the course. The '70s began with Mickey Wright retiring from full-time competition at the age of 34 and with JoAnne Carner, one of golf's best amateurs, a five-time winner of the Women's Amateur title, turning pro at the age of 30. She had already won a professional tournament as an amateur, the last to do so, and would win 42 more, including two U.S. Women's Opens, in the next 15 years.

It was the time of Jack Nicklaus, Lee Trevino, Gary Player and Tom Watson. Nicklaus won eight major championships during the '70s and, in 1971, became the first player to win all the majors twice. By 1978 he would be the first and only to win all of them three times. Trevino won four majors — he also won the U.S., Canadian and British Opens in a four-week stretch in 1971. Player won four majors during the decade. Watson won the British Open in 1975. In 1977 he began an incredible six-year streak in which he won 26 times in the United States, including two Masters and a U.S. Open, plus four more British Opens. The first of those was in 1977 at Turnberry in the storied 36-hole shootout with Nicklaus. He was the

FROM LEFT: THE LYNX 1.80 JUMBO, THE HOGAN 392, AND THE PENFOLD ACE

1990s

...

*In 1990, the R&A adopted the 1.68-inch American-size
ball, which thus became standard
throughout the world.*

...

*For the first time, in the 1996 revision, the words
"slow play" appeared in the Rules of Golf.*

...

*In 1997, Callaway Golf announced the hiring of
Chuck Yash, its planned entry into the golf ball
business and the retirement of Ely Callaway.
Only two of the three happened.*

...

*Tiger Woods won his third consecutive U.S. Amateur
in 1996, then turned professional and won twice on
the PGA Tour to earn Rookie of the Year honors.*

...

*In 1997, Tiger Woods won the Masters by a record
12 strokes. Jack Nicklaus competed in his
150th consecutive major championship at the
U.S. Open at Congressional.*

...

leading money-winner from '77 through '80, then again in '84, when he won three more tournaments. He was named Player of the Year six times over that span.

It was the time of Johnny Miller, whose meteoric career blazed briefly but intensely. He fired a final-round 63 to win the 1973 U.S. Open at Oakmont, then won 14 more times in the next 32 months, including eight in 1974. He won the 1976 British Open playing graphite shafts, becoming the first to win with them in a major, and a Surlyn ball. It was, briefly, the time of Tom Weiskopf, who won five tournaments, including the British Open, in a two-month stretch in 1973. That same year, Kathy Whitworth was the LPGA Player of the Year for the seventh time in eight years. Sandra Haynie won the Women's Open, the LPGA Championship and four other tournaments in 1974 on her way to 42 career victories and the Hall of Fame. Judy Rankin won seven tournaments and an LPGA record $150,734 in 1976, the first player to top $100,000 in a season, won the Vare Trophy and was named Player of the Year. The next year she won five tournaments and $122,890 and again was the Vare and Player of the Year winner. And it was the beginning of a Hall of

Fame career for Nancy Lopez. She won five tournaments in a row and nine overall in 1978, her rookie season, recharging the LPGA Tour in the process.

Deane Beman, a success as an amateur, an insurance executive and a PGA Tour professional, became commissioner of the Tour in 1974. Over the next 20 years, he would lead it to unprecedented growth. Also in 1974, the inaugural Tournament Players Championship was played. In 1979 it would move to the Tournament Players Club at Sawgrass, a controversial Pete Dye design, the first "stadium course" and the first in the PGA Tour's ever-growing network of TPC courses.

The 1977 U.S. Open was the first tournament in the United States to provide coverage of all 18 holes. In the meantime, CBS director Frank Chirkinian was defining television coverage of golf, especially at the Masters Tournament in Augusta.

Separated by several years and more than a quarter million miles, there were two other remarkable occurrences in the '70s. In 1971, Alan Shepard hit two shots on the moon with a modified 6-iron. In 1977, Al Geiberger became the first in PGA Tour history to break 60, record-ing a 59 in the second round of the Danny Thomas Memphis Classic. After opening with a 72 and closing with rounds of 72 and 70, Geiberger became an automatic trivia question — the only man to shoot 15 under par in a a 72-hole tournament without a round in the 60s.

He also violated a time-honored Tour practice of alternating balls throughout the round. Once his Hogan started going in the hole with regularity, he stuck with it all the way, then shipped it to the Hall of Fame.

Fred Raphael was the man responsible for the original Shell's Wonderful World of Golf, which aired for the last time in 1971. Seven years later, Raphael came up with another hit in the Legends of Golf, a better-ball event for seniors that was televised by NBC. Sam Snead and Gardner Dickinson won in 1978. The next year, as the largest television audience of the golf year watched in wonder, Roberto de Vicenzo and Julius Boros beat Tommy Bolt and Art Wall Jr. in a six-hole playoff, the teams matching birdies until the final hole.

The USGA announced that it would conduct a Senior Open beginning in 1980, and the Senior Tour was born.

THE TOP FLITE XL 2000 BY SPALDING

A Ball for You and Me and Everybody Else

THE STORY OF GOLF BALLS IN THE LAST 20 YEARS OF THE 20TH CENTURY is a tale of dimples and distance, covers and colors and customization... and no little confusion in the marketplace. As companies fought for market share, their research and development departments produced every conceivable — and some inconceivable — variation of core design, dimple design and cover material in an attempt to make balls for every variety of player. All the claims promised accuracy, spin, control, feel and usually durability.

But the biggest carrot was almost always more distance, the goal that has always tantalized every golfer short of the professionals tours... and most of them, too. That led to the conviction — perception might be a better word — in certain circles that the ball was going too far and outmoding golf courses. This was not a new perception, of course. Doomsayers had been singing the same song since the turn of the century. But the intensity of the outcry was enough to keep the powers-that-be wondering what to do about it for a couple of decades.

Perhaps the most radical geometric departure in dimple design ever came from Dunlop in 1981 with the introduction of the Maxfli DDH. It was so named because the cover was dotted with 360 dimples of four different sizes arranged in a dodecahedron pattern, a configuration of 12 pentagonal or five-sided shapes that fit neatly around the surface of the ball. Not only was the dodecahedron pattern new, the DDH was the only ball in modern times with dimples of more than one size. Developed by Dunlop in England, its makers claimed the ball was longer, of course, and more accurate. It held the only patent covering structural configuration to be issued on a golf ball for at least 10 years, except for the unapproved Polara ball.

One problem in ball design is that with the compression molding process, covers must be molded onto the center in halves, creating a seam that theoretically disrupts uniformity and disturbs airflow in flight. Dunlop felt it had solved that problem with the DDH by creating nine artificial seams that, along with the natural seam, crisscrossed the surface and divided it into those 12 identical pentagonal areas, thus presenting repeatable surfaces to the air no matter on which axis the ball was spinning.

Dunlop called the DDH "the golf ball perfected." Titleist's Dr. John Jepson, one of golf's most knowledgeable scientists, demurred, declaring, "There are certain things you can continue to do with dimples to affect trajectory and customize balls to the individual player. We have continually stressed that golfers should experiment with a variety of balls and see which one or ones suit their own games." Some 19 years later, that was still being stressed.

Colored balls made a comeback in 1981. Wilson's orange Pro-Staff was joined the next year by yellow balls from PGA Golf and an orange sphere from Ram. The claim, and there is substantiation for it, is that bright yellow and orange colors are more vivid than white under dim conditions. Eventually there was a multitude of different-colored balls on the market, used mostly by women, although Hale Irwin and Jerry Pate played the Wilson orange ball and Wayne Levi won the 1982 Hawaiian Open with it. All, of course, were on the Wilson staff. Interest in colors eventually waned, and Wilson was left with a warehouse of unsold oranges.

The distance and dimple race heated up again in late 1982 when Titleist introduced its 384 Tour ball, named, logically, after the number of dimples on its cover. Tour players loved it, calling it the hottest ball they had ever played, and for the next seven years it was the most popular ball among the playing professionals. Even Jack Nicklaus played it in several spring and early summer tournaments in 1983, despite the fact that he owned the MacGregor Company that made a competing pro-line ball that bore Nicklaus's name. "I was losing 20 to 40 yards to the other fellas," Nicklaus said. Other MacGregor staff members on Tour followed suit. By early June, however, just in time for the U.S. Open, MacGregor came out with

TOP ROW FROM LEFT: THE TITLEIST, THE MAXFLI ELITE   BOTTOM ROW FROM LEFT: WILSON STAFF SMART-CORE, THE NIKE DISTANCE

its new Jack Nicklaus Muirfield ball sporting 392 dimples. Nicklaus and the other staff players called it "awesome" and put it in their bags. Other manufacturers soon came on the scene with a bunch of dimples on their balls. The AMF/Ben Hogan Company produced a Hogan 392 in both a Surlyn and balata. Ram introduced its Tour 400, also with 392 dimples. The more dimples the merrier was the theme of the moment.

Nicklaus said his new MacGregor ball was going 14 yards farther than the old one when tested on a machine. And he was worried that the game was going to suffer because of it. "I'm nowhere as long as I was in the '60s, but I'm hitting the ball just as far," he said. "I've gone from not being able to reach any of the par-5s in two to being able to reach all of them. I've told the USGA that I think the balls are going too far and that it has to pull them back. It's wrong for the game of golf." Nicklaus, then a part owner of MacGregor, even commissioned veteran ball designer Troy Puckett to develop a ball that would go only half as far as a normal ball. Puckett did, producing a one-piece model in 1989, and Jack built a short course in the Cayman Islands to accommodate the ball. Savings in

land, cost and time were the obvious benefits. There were a few short courses built around the United States, but the idea never caught on. In fact, Nicklaus's average driving distance in 1983 was 266.1 yards, three yards *shorter* than in 1980 before the spate of so-called hot balls appeared. The Tour's median driving distance in 1983 was 259.4, almost three yards longer than in 1982 but a half-yard shorter than in 1981. In 1998 the average on Tour was 270.6. The doomsayers pointed to numbers like that and cried again to restrict the distance the ball can travel, and there were many within and without the USGA who did so. But they ignored the fact, as they had ignored it for years, that there was that Overall Distance Standard beyond which no ball could or did travel.

And they ignored the fact that golfers at the highest amateur and professional levels were getting bigger and stronger, were better-conditioned, better-fed and better-taught than at any time in history. Courses were groomed better, fairways were firmer and faster. Yes, equipment was better. Clubs were designed to work more efficiently. Balls were more consistent through the dozen. Yet, as technical director Frank Thomas pointed out in 1994,

2000

• • •

*The feared Y2K bug failed to materialize after the
United States spent an estimated $100 billion to
stave off potential problems. The New Year came in
glitchlessly, and as far as we know, no rounds of golf
were interrupted at the stroke of midnight.*

• • •

*Tiger Woods won his first two tournaments of the
year, running his streak of consecutive victories to
six. He won twice more through May, then romped
to a record 15-stroke victory in the
U.S. Open at Pebble Beach.*

• • •

*Under contract to play Titleist clubs and balls,
Woods switched to the new Nike ball
and won the Open.*

• • •

USGA statistics kept over the previous 25 years showed that average winning score in a Tour event had improved about one stroke per round. Thomas credited that to better putting, partly because of better-conditioned greens. And as the 20th century loomed, nobody had bettered Byron Nelson's scoring average of 68.33 established 55 years earlier over courses that were shorter but also in much poorer condition.

There was no question heading into the '80s that the competition at Tour level was getting better and deeper. One reason was that international players were getting better and were starting to make an impact on the world scene. There are some who claim, justifiably, that the worldwide switch to the 1.68 ball was a big influence. But probably the biggest factor was Severiano Ballesteros.

Seve won the British Open as a 22-year-old in 1979. In the '80s he would win two more British Opens and two Masters, blazing across the world golf scene with flair and fervor, lifting the European Tour to prominence and the European Ryder Cup team to parity with a United States team that had dominated over the years.

Perhaps his most significant contribution was to

show European golfers they could win in international competition. The likes of Sandy Lyle, Bernhard Langer, Nick Faldo, Ian Woosnam and Jose Maria Olazabal would win major championships over the next two decades, and more and more quality players were pouring out of Europe (not to mention the rest of the world) to challenge American supremacy.

Greg Norman was one from the rest of the world. The dashing Australian, who took up golf late, turned professional in 1976 at the age of 21 and by the turn of the century had won 18 events on the U.S. Tour and another 56, including two British Opens, around the world.

At 40 and presumably finished after a 1979 season that was the worst of his career, Jack Nicklaus came back a year later to win his fourth U.S. Open with a record 272 at Baltusrol and his fifth PGA Championship. In 1986, at 46, he won his sixth Masters title. In 1998, at 58 and troubled by a bad hip that would need replacement surgery early the next year, he tied for sixth in the Masters, becoming the oldest player ever to finish in the top 10. By then he had won 10 times in a sparse Senior Tour schedule. Eight of those were major championships.

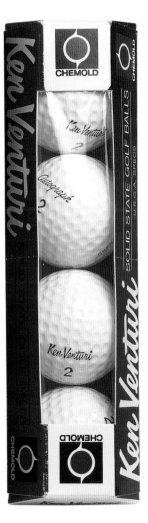

Nicklaus had a shot at another major in 1982 until Tom Watson chipped in from the rough on the 71st hole at Pebble Beach to beat Jack by a stroke and win his only U.S. Open. Watson later won the British Open to become one of only five players to win both in the same year, then added his fifth British Open crown in 1983.

In 1982, Julie Simpson became the first player in almost 50 years to win three straight U.S. Women's Amateurs. As Julie Inkster, she would go on to 22 professional victories through 1999, a year in which she won the U.S. Open and the LPGA, to give her a total of five majors, a career Grand Slam and a berth in the Hall of Fame. Inkster was one of a cadre of eventual Hall of Fame players who battled for supremacy over the last 20 years of the century — Nancy Lopez, Beth Daniel, Betsy King, JoAnne Carner, Patty Sheehan, Pat Bradley, Amy Alcott, Donna Caponi, and Hollis Stacey, who won three U.S. Women's Opens. Sweden's Annika Sorenstam came along in 1994, and beginning in 1995 she won 18 tournaments, including two Women's Opens, in five years, adding another at the start of 2000 and breezing into the Hall of Fame. But soon she found herself in a battle with Australian Karrie

Webb, who won 16 times from 1995 through 1999. In 1999 she won six tournaments and an LPGA record $1,591,959. Then she won her first three tournaments of 2000 and began looking like the best woman player ever.

In 1988, Curtis Strange, aided by a U.S. Open victory at The Country Club and three other wins, became the first to top $1 million on the PGA Tour with a $1,147,644 total, marking his third year in the last four as leading money winner. The next year he repeated his Open victory at Oak Hill, the first to win them back-to-back since Ben Hogan in 1950 and 1951. But it was to be the last of Strange's 17 career Tour victories.

In 1989, Tom Kite broke Strange's record with three victories and $1,395,278 in winnings that made him the Tour's all-time leading money winner, a spot he held until late in 1995. It also earned him his second Player of the Year award. Jay Sigel, who had won the 1979 British Amateur, added three Mid-Amateur titles to two U.S. Amateur crowns in the '80s. The quintessential amateur, he turned professional in 1993 and began a successful Senior Tour career. Don January and Miller Barber dominated the early years of the Senior Tour, Barber winning

three U.S. Senior Opens and two other senior majors from 1981 through 1985. Peter Thomson won a record nine tournaments in 1985, but Chi Chi Rodriguez, Bob Charles, Bruce Crampton and Gary Player were the consistently best players through the late '80s and early '90s.

Jim Colbert, Mike Hill and Dave Stockton would have been the dominant players in the '90s had it not been for Lee Trevino and Hale Irwin. Trevino came on board full-time in 1990 and won 28 times, a Senior Tour record, in the next nine years. Irwin won his third U.S. Open title in 1990, becoming, at the age of 45, the oldest man to win that championship. Five years later he joined the seniors and won 25 tournaments in his first four and a half years, including a record-tying nine victories in 1997 and seven more in 1998, along with a record $2,861,945 in winnings. In both years he fended off Gil Morgan, who won six each season. In 1999, Bruce Fleisher, who had won only once in a lengthy PGA Tour career, did it seven times in his rookie senior season and became the new sheriff in town.

Arnold Palmer, who won the 1980 Senior Open in his "rookie" season, won four more majors through 1985. He played his final U.S. Open in 1994 in an emotional farewell, but in 2000, at the age of 70, he still was playing in the Masters and competing on the Senior Tour.

In 1985, the European Ryder Cup team, captained by Tony Jacklin, beat the United States for the first time since 1957 at The Belfry in England. Two years later it would win for the first time ever on U.S. soil, beating a Jack Nicklaus-captained team on Nicklaus's own course at Muirfield Village in Ohio. From that time on, the biennial matches were a war.

In 1987, Judy Bell became the first woman elected to the USGA Executive Committee. In 1996, she would become the first female president of the organization.

The game was growing almost exponentially. In 1961, there were 5 million golfers in the United States. By the mid-'80s there were 20 million players and more than 12,000 courses in the country. By 1999, there were more than 16,000 courses and more than 25 million golfers.

The 1990s were eventful. Hall Thompson, founder of Shoal Creek, site of the 1990 PGA Championship, admitted that the club had no black members because that sort of thing wasn't done in Birmingham, Alabama. The PGA and the PGA Tour announced they would not play tournaments at clubs that had no black or women members. Many clubs around the country, including Augusta National, hastened to comply. In 1990, Spalding and Titleist announced the settlement of a bevy of lawsuits that had been flying back and forth since 1981 over various design and production patents.

The first Solheim Cup matches, the female version of the Ryder Cup, were played in 1990, inspired by, funded by and named for Ping's inventor. The President's Cup, a competition that matched U.S. professionals against those from the rest of the world, excluding Europe, followed in 1994.

Lefthander Phil Mickelson won the U.S. Amateur and National Collegiate titles in 1990, the first to do so since Nicklaus, and went on to star as a professional. Chip Beck shot the second 59 in a Tour event in 1991, but on an inferior course in the Las Vegas Invitational. Also in 1991, the USGA attempted to make handicaps more portable by introducing the Slope System, which adjusted handicaps according to the difficulty of the course being played. Almost 20 years earlier, it had introduced Equitable Stroke Control, which restricted the number of

TOP ROW FROM LEFT: TITLEIST 304 TOUR, NICKLAUS CHAMPION, MAXFLI XS TOUR
BOTTOM ROW FROM LEFT: SLAZENGER 420s SELECT, SLAZENGER RAW-DISTANCE, ULTRA 500

TOP ROW FROM LEFT: HOGAN 2PCE. DISTANCE, TOP FLITE AERO, TAYLOR MADE INERGEL
BOTTOM ROW FROM LEFT: STRATA, PRECEPT EV, PRECEPT MC

Tiger

• • •

*If there had been any doubts as the 2000 season
progressed that Tiger Woods was the best player in the
world, he laid them firmly to rest with the two greatest
performances in major championship golf. In doing so he
became, at 24, the youngest player and only the fifth in
history to complete the career Grand Slam.*

*After winning four tournaments before the end of May,
Woods stunned the golf world by lapping the U.S. Open
field at fearsome Pebble Beach by an astonishing
15 strokes, the largest winning margin ever.
His score of 12-under-par 272 matched the best 72-hole
score in history and marked the first time anybody
had finished in double digits under par
(actually, he was 16 under, because the USGA changed
the par-5 second hole to a par 4).*

*The best was yet to come. Five weeks later, at the
British Open on the hallowed Old Course at St. Andrews,
Woods marched inexorably to a 19-under-par 269 and
victory by eight strokes. It was the lowest score in
relation to par in major championship history.*

*Woods thus joined Gene Sarazen, Ben Hogan, Gary
Player and Jack Nicklaus as the only players to win the
four major professional championships: the Masters,
U.S. Open, British Open and PGA Championship.
Nicklaus previously had been the youngest to
accomplish this at the age of 26.*

And, he did it with a Nike ball.

• • •

strokes that players at the various handicap levels could take on an individual hole. In 1994, Tim Finchem succeeded Deane Beman as commissioner of the PGA Tour. That same year, a company called Softspikes, Inc., introduced a soon-to-be-popular plastic substitute for the metal spike that would eliminate spike marks and greatly improve the quality of green surfaces. David Duvall, in his third year on Tour, won his first tournament in 1997 and crammed 10 more titles into the next 19 months. After a final-round 59, the third in Tour history, that gave him victory in the 1999 Bob Hope Classic, he briefly was heralded as the best player in the world.

But the '90s eventually belonged to Tiger Woods, both the amateur and professional version. He won three straight USGA Junior Championships and three straight U.S. Amateur Championships. He turned professional in late 1996 and by the end of 1999 had won 18 tournaments, including the Masters in 1997 and the PGA in 1999. He won his last four tournaments in 1999 and his first two in 2000 to tie Ben Hogan for the second-best streak in history. At that point, he was clearly the dominant player in golf.

In the meantime, golf balls had been multiplying at an even more bewildering pace than Tiger Woods victories. By the end of the '90s, there were almost 2,000 variations of balls on the USGA conforming list. Less than half of those would make it to market, but enough did to make most consumers scratch their heads when it came to making a choice.

With the expiration of the basic Surlyn patent, companies began to mix and match cover ingredients to modify hardness and softness. In 1986, Spalding introduced a new cover material it called Zinthane, a blend of two types of Surlyn, and put it on its high-spin Tour Edition ball. Five years later it introduced Zylin, supposedly a rival to balata for soft feel, and eventually the company returned with Zinthane II. The Titleist HVC, the first two-piece ball to bear the name, came out in 1991 with a Lithium Surlyn cover. Soon all the companies were experimenting with all kinds of elastomers, polymers, ionomers and the like. Titanium, tungsten and magnesium became hot items in the '90s, both inside and outside the ball.

Inner ball construction was changing as well. In 1996, Spalding introduced multi-layer technology in its

The Cayman Ball was designed to travel only half the distance of regular balls in an effort to address potential real estate problems around the world. Concept was championed by Jack Nicklaus, and designed by Troy Puckett. There are about 20 "Cayman" courses around the world. The ball is still manufactured today.

Strata ball, placing an additional mantle layer between the core and the cover. This was to enhance distance, spin and feel. Titleist followed suit in 1998 with its HP Distance ball, and soon double-cover technology became commonplace. Titleist also launched its HP Eclipse in 2000, touting it as a dual-*core* ball. Bridgestone's Precept Tour model was a *four*-piece ball.

The Precept EV was dubbed the "smart ball" on the premise that because of a graduated density of the core, from softer at the outside to firmer in the center, it would work efficiently with any clubhead speed. But that didn't stop Bridgestone from making other models. In 1998, Precept had 23 victories on the four major professional tours with six different balls.

Dimpling was not being ignored either. Number, design and even shape were all over the lot. The number of dimples on various brands in 1999 ranged from 332 on the Top-Flite Aero to 500 on several Wilson balls. Most dimples were spherical, but the Aero's were both teardrop- and ellipsoid-shaped. Wilson's Staff Straight Distance ball had an ellipsoid dimple pattern. Titleist used both icosahedral and quadrilateral patterns in its line.

Spalding even re-introduced the over-sized ball, the 1.72-inch Magna that is still in its Top-Flite XL 2000 line. In 1990, the Nite-Lite glow-in-the-dark ball was introduced, just in case anybody was interested in golf after midnight. All this in an attempt to make a ball, or balls, as it were, for everybody. And there *was* something for everybody. If you wanted distance, you perhaps went for the Slazenger Raw Distance with its dual radius dimples and a titanium core that its makers said was yards longer than any other ball. Or if you wanted feel and spin, Slazenger offered its Pro Preferred. In between, for both distance and control, there was the Slazenger DC Tour.

Simple enough, except that every manufacturer was making the same claims with its line of balls, usually an extensive line. By 1998, Spalding had 13 varieties of Top-Flites and three Strata models on the market. In 1999, obviously recognizing the clutter and attempting to rectify it somewhat, the company reduced its Top-Flite brand names from eight to two — Top-Flite XL 2000 and Top-Flite XL. Still, there are six versions of the XL 2000 brand and two of the XL. Plus the company still has three varieties of Strata.

For 2000, Titleist had nine Titleist models, plus the Pinnacle line. It also dispensed a CD-ROM that theoretically provided a customer with the means to determine which particular ball was for him or her.

By now, some premium balls were priced at more than $50 a dozen, although prices ranged down to the low $20s (and even lower if you went to your local discount store). And the balls kept coming as the century wound down. Taylor Made, whose metal woods had swept the market 20 years before, introduced its InerGel multi-layered ball. Cobra, also a top-ranked club company that had been recently acquired by Titleist parent Fortune Brands, came out with two double-cover balls. Nike, barely in the golf shoe business before it signed Tiger woods to a lucrative contract, came on the market with five new balls.

SP Golf introduced three models of the Bald Eagle, a ball that had six symmetrically placed smooth spots on its surface to enhance putter contact. SP's theory was that if your putter caught a dimple at a certain angle, it could produce adverse sidespin.

In 1999, an advertisement for Titleist's HP2 balls put it best, probably unwittingly. It illustrated a ball with

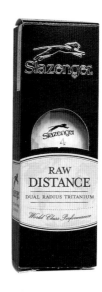

a "high velocity polybutadiene core, soft Hytrel® inner mantle layer, responsive, cut-proof Lithium Surlyn® cover, 440 cuboctahedron dimple pattern." The punch line: "You don't need a Ph.D. in astrophysics to appreciate Titleist HP2. (But it wouldn't hurt.)"

Callaway, the leading premium club-seller in the world in the '90s, leaped into the ball business in early 2000. It hired Chuck Yash, a veteran of the ball business with Spalding and at that time president of Taylor Made, and invested three and a half years and $160 million in the project. It emerged with a ball and a marketing ploy obviously aimed at taking advantage of the confusion in the marketplace. It introduced two varieties of its ball, one with a firm feel, the other with a soft feel. The company refused to discuss the technology (the ball had dual covers around a solid core) and claimed the two versions were comparable in performance.

"We know there is a lot of complex science that goes into making a golf ball, but we don't think there should be a lot of complexity to buying one," said Ely Callaway, the company's founder.

"We've deliberately made the choice simple for the

golfer to make," Yash said. "We've combined all of the performance benefits into one ball so players no longer need to sacrifice control for distance or feel for durability. Each ball contains a unique synergy of distance, control, spin, feel and durability characteristics. This eliminates the confusion and guesswork in trying to identify the golf ball that is right for each individual golfer."

Callaway's packaging concept also was a departure from the traditional. Heretofore, balls had been packaged in sleeves of three and boxes of a dozen, occasionally 15. Callaway boxed its balls in five-ball sleeves, 10-ball packs and 20-ball packages. That was based on somebody's survey that indicated the average golfer used 4.5 balls per round. The packaging also was clean, bearing none of the hype that covered most other companies' boxes. Instead, imprinted on each plastic sleeve were homilies such as "Look for a fourth. Find a friend for life." or "Smile. You're about to golf." The ball's name also was unique. It was Rule 35 (there were only 34 in the Rules of Golf), which Callaway said was "Enjoy the game."

Despite the proliferation and confusion, millions around the world were doing just that. Whatever ball any-

body chose, whether it was exactly the "right" one, it was a lot better than the featherie of more than 500 years before. The game had come a long way. As with everything from toasters to automobiles to airplanes and beyond, technology had made golf better... and therefore more fun. And while there had been wonderful improvements in clubheads and shafts over the centuries, along with great advancements in agronomy and course design, the biggest difference in making the game more playable had come as a result of enhancements to the ball.

How far would Tiger Woods hit a featherie? Certainly farther than Allan Robertson and Old Tom Morris. But until we come up with a vintage featherie from half a millennium ago and put it to the test, no one will know for sure. Nor should we care. Today's highly groomed courses demand the precision of high-tech clubs and balls. A featherie would not be suitable for the greens at Augusta National, nor for your local munies.

Still, the nature and challenge of golf had not changed over the centuries — you struck some sort of ball with some sort of club until you got it into some sort of hole.

And thank God for the rabbits. ●

The Golf Ball Rules

In 1774 the Honourable Company of Edinburgh Golfers issued the first set of 13 rules for golf, but the Royal and Ancient of St. Andrews eventually became the ruling body of British golf. In 1895, the U.S. Golf Association was formed and became the rules-making body for the United States. The two approved a uniform set of Rules in 1952, although the ball size remained different until 1990. Shown here are only those rules that directly concern the golf ball.

RULE 5
THE BALL

5-1   GENERAL

The ball the player uses shall conform to requirements specified in Appendix III on maximum weight, minimum size, spherical symmetry, initial velocity and overall distance.

Note: The Committee may require, in the conditions of a competition (Rule 33-1), that the ball the player uses must be named on the current List of Conforming Golf Balls issued by the United States Golf Association.

5-2   FOREIGN MATERIAL

Foreign material must not be applied to a ball for the purpose of changing its playing characteristics.

Penalty for Breach of Rule 5-1 or 5-2
Disqualification.

5-3   BALL UNFIT FOR PLAY

A ball is unfit for play if it is visibly cut, cracked or out of shape. A ball is not unfit for play solely because mud or other materials adhere to it, its surface is scratched or scraped or its paint is damaged or discolored.

If a player has reason to believe his ball has become unfit for play during the play of the hole being played, he may during the play of such hole lift his ball without penalty to determine whether it is unfit.

Before lifting the ball, the player must announce his intention to his opponent in match play or his marker or a fellow-competitor in stroke play and mark the position of the ball. He may then lift and examine the ball without cleaning it and must give his opponent, marker or fellow-competitor an opportunity to examine the ball.

If he fails to comply with this procedure, he shall incur a penalty of one stroke.

If it is determined that the ball has become unfit for play during play of the hole being played, the player may substitute another ball, placing it on the spot where the original ball lay. Otherwise, the original ball shall be replaced.

If a ball breaks into pieces as a result of a stroke, the stroke shall be cancelled and the player shall play a ball without penalty as nearly as possible at the spot from which the original ball was played — see Rule 20-5.

Penalty for Breach of Rule
Match play: Loss of hole.
Stroke play: Two strokes.

If a player incurs the general penalty for breach of Rule 5-3, no additional penalty under the Rule shall be applied.

Note: If the opponent, marker or fellow-competitor wishes to dispute a claim of unfitness, he must do so before the player plays another ball.

RULE 12
SEARCHING FOR AND IDENTIFYING BALL

Definitions:
A "hazard" is any bunker or water hazard.

A "bunker" is a hazard consisting of a prepared area of ground, often a hollow, from which turf or soil has been removed and replaced with sand or the like. Grass-covered ground bordering or within a bunker is not part of the bunker. The margin of a bunker extends vertically downwards, but not upwards. A ball is in a bunker when it lies in or any part of it touches the bunker.

A "water hazard" is any sea, lake, pond, river, ditch, surface drainage ditch or other open water course (whether or not containing water) and anything of a similar nature.

All ground or water within the margin of a water hazard is part of the water hazard. The margin of a water hazard extends vertically upwards and downwards. Stakes and lines defining the margins of water hazards are in the hazards. Such stakes are obstructions. A ball is in a water hazard when it lies in or any part of it touches the water hazard.

12-1   SEARCHING FOR BALL; SEEING BALL

In searching for his ball anywhere on the course, the player may touch or bend long grass, rushes, bushes, whins, heather or the like, but only to the extent necessary to find and identify it, provided that this does not improve the lie of the ball, the area of his intended swing or his line of play.

A player is not necessarily entitled to see his ball when playing a stroke.

In a hazard, if a ball is covered by loose impediments or sand, the player may remove by probing, raking or other means as much thereof as will enable him to see a part of the ball. If an excess is removed, no penalty is incurred and the ball shall be re-covered so that only a part of the ball is visible. If the ball is moved in such removal, no penalty is incurred; the ball shall be replaced and, if necessary, re-covered. As to removal of loose impediments outside a hazard, see Rule 23.

If a ball lying in casual water, ground under repair or a hole, cast or runway made by a burrowing animal, a reptile or a bird is accidentally moved during search, no penalty is incurred; the ball shall be replaced, unless the player elects to proceed under Rule 25-1b.

If a ball is believed to be lying in water in a water hazard, the player may probe for it with a club or otherwise. If the ball is moved in so doing, no penalty is incurred; the ball shall be replaced, unless the player elects to proceed under Rule 26-1.

Penalty for Breach of Rule 12-1
Match play: Loss of hole.
Stroke play: Two strokes.

12-2   IDENTIFYING BALL

The responsibility for playing the proper ball rests with the player. Each player should put an identification mark on his ball.

Except in a hazard, the player may, without penalty, lift a ball he believes to be his own for the purpose of identification and clean it to the extent necessary for identification. If the ball is the player's ball, he shall replace it. Before lifting the ball, the player must announce his intention to his opponent in match play or his marker or a fellow-competitor in stroke play and mark the position of the ball. He must then give his opponent, marker or fellow-competitor an opportunity to observe the lifting and replacement. If he lifts his ball without announcing his intention in advance, marking the position of the ball or giving his opponent, marker or fellow-competitor an opportunity to observe, or if he lifts his ball for identification in a hazard, or cleans it more than necessary for identification, he shall incur a penalty of one stroke and the ball shall be replaced.

If a player who is required to replace a ball fails to do so, he shall incur the penalty for a breach of Rule 20-3a, but no additional penalty under Rule 12-2 shall be applied.

RULE 13

BALL PLAYED AS IT LIES; LIE, AREA OF INTENDED SWING AND LINE OF PLAY; STANCE

Definitions:

A "hazard" is any bunker or water hazard.

A "bunker" is a hazard consisting of a prepared area of ground, often a hollow, from which turf or soil has been removed and replaced with sand or the like. Grass-covered ground bordering or within a bunker is not part of the bunker. The margin of a bunker extends vertically downwards, but not upwards. A ball is in a bunker when it lies in or any part of it touches the bunker.

A "water hazard" is any sea, lake, pond, river, ditch, surface drainage ditch or other open water course (whether or not containing water) and anything of a similar nature.

All ground or water within the margin of a water hazard is part of the water hazard. The margin of a water hazard extends vertically upwards and downwards. Stakes and lines defining the margins of water hazards are in the hazards. Such stakes are obstructions. A ball is in a water hazard when it lies in or any part of it touches the water hazard.

The "line of play" is the direction which the player wishes his ball to take after a stroke, plus a reasonable distance on either side of the intended direction. The line of play extends vertically upwards from the ground, but does not extend beyond the hole.

13-1   BALL PLAYED AS IT LIES

The ball shall be played as it lies, except as otherwise provided in the Rules. (Ball at rest moved — see Rule 18.)

13-2   IMPROVING LIE, AREA OF INTENDED SWING OR LINE OF PLAY

Except as provided in the Rules, a player shall not improve or allow to be improved: the position or lie of his ball, the area of his intended swing, his line of play or a reasonable extension of that line beyond the hole or the area in which he is to drop or place a ball by any of the following actions:

moving, bending or breaking anything growing or fixed (including immovable obstructions and objects defining out of bounds) or removing or pressing down sand, loose soil, replaced divots, other cut turf placed in position or other irregularities of surface except as follows: as may occur in fairly taking his stance,in making a stroke or the backward movement of his club for a stroke, on the teeing ground in creating or eliminating irregularities of surface, or on the putting green in removing sand and loose soil as provided in Rule 16-1a or in repairing damage as provided in Rule 16-1c.

The club may be grounded only lightly and shall not be pressed on the ground.

Exception:
Ball in hazard — see Rule 13-4.

13-3   BUILDING STANCE

A player is entitled to place his feet firmly in taking his stance, but he shall not build a stance.

13-4   BALL IN HAZARD

Except as provided in the Rules, before making a stroke at a ball which is in a hazard (whether a bunker or a water hazard) or which, having been lifted from a hazard, may be dropped or placed in the hazard, the player shall not:
a. Test the condition of the hazard or any similar hazard,
b. Touch the ground in the hazard or water in the water hazard with a club or otherwise, or
c. Touch or move a loose impediment lying in or touching the hazard.

Exceptions:
1. Provided nothing is done which constitutes testing the condition of the hazard or improves the lie of the ball, there is no penalty if the player (a) touches the ground in any hazard or water in a water hazard as a result of or to prevent falling, in removing an obstruction, in measuring or in retrieving or lifting a ball under any Rule or (b) places his clubs in a hazard.

2. The player after playing the stroke, or his caddie at any time without the authority of the player, may smooth sand or soil in the hazard, provided that, if the ball is still in the hazard, nothing is done which improves the lie of the ball or assists the player in his subsequent play of the hole.

Note:
At any time, including at address or in the backward movement for the stroke, the player may touch with a club or otherwise any obstruction, any construction declared by the Committee to be an integral part of the course or any grass, bush, tree or other growing thing.

Penalty For Breach of Rule
Match play: Loss of hole.
Stroke play: Two strokes.
(Searching for ball — see Rule 12-1.)

RULE 14

STRIKING THE BALL

Definition:
A "stroke" is the forward movement of the club made with the intention of fairly striking at and moving the ball, but if a player checks his downswing voluntarily before the clubhead reaches the ball he is deemed not to have made a stroke.

14-1   BALL TO BE FAIRLY STRUCK AT

The ball shall be fairly struck at with the head of the club and must not be pushed, scraped or spooned.

14-2   ASSISTANCE

In making a stroke, a player shall not accept physical assistance or protection from the elements.

Penalty for Breach of Rule 14-1or -2
Match play: Loss of hole.
Stroke play: Two strokes.

14-3   ARTIFICIAL DEVICES AND UNUSUAL EQUIPMENT

A player in doubt as to whether use of an item would constitute a breach of Rule 14-3 should consult the United States Golf Association.

A manufacturer may suit to the United States Golf Association a sample of an item which is to be manufactured for a ruling as to whether its use during a stipulated round would cause a player to be in breach of Rule 14-3. Such sample will become the property of the United States Golf Association for reference purposes. If a manufacturer fails to suit a sample before manufacturing and/or marketing the item, he assumes the risk of a ruling that use of the item would be contrary to the Rules of Golf.

Except as provided in the Rules, during a stipulated round the player shall not use any artificial device or unusual equipment:

a. Which might assist him in making a stroke or in his play; or

b. For the purpose of gauging or measuring distance or conditions which might affect his play; or

c. Which might assist him in gripping the club, except that:

(i) plain gloves may be worn;

(ii) resin, powder and drying or moisturizing agents may be used;

(iii) tape or gauze may be applied to the grip (provided such application does not render the grip non-conforming under Rule 4-1c); and

(iv) a towel or handkerchief may be wrapped around the grip.

Penalty for Breach of Rule 14-3
Disqualification.

14-4   STRIKING THE BALL MORE THAN ONCE

If a player's club strikes the ball more than once in the course of a stroke, the player shall count the stroke and add a penalty stroke, making two strokes in all.

14-5   PLAYING MOVING BALL

A player shall not play while his ball is moving.

Exceptions:
Ball falling off tee — Rule 11-3.
Striking the ball more than once — Rule 14-4.
Ball moving in water — Rule 14-6.

When the ball begins to move only after the player has begun the stroke or the backward movement of his club for the stroke, he shall incur no penalty under this Rule for playing a moving ball, but he is not exempt from any penalty incurred under the following Rules:
Ball at rest moved by player — Rule 18-2a.
Ball at rest moving after address — Rule 18-2b.
Ball at rest moving after loose impediment touched — Rule 18-2c.
(Ball purposely deflected or stopped by player, partner or caddie — see Rule 1-2.)

14-6   BALL MOVING IN WATER

When a ball is moving in water in a water hazard, the player may, without penalty, make a stroke, but he must not delay making his stroke in order to allow the wind or current to improve the position of the ball. A ball moving in water in a water hazard may be lifted if the player elects to invoke Rule 26.

Penalty for Breach of Rule 14-5 or -6
Match play: Loss of hole.
Stroke play: Two strokes.

RULE 15
WRONG BALL; SUBSTITUTED BALL

Definition:
A "wrong ball" is any ball other than the player's:
a. Ball in play,
b. Provisional ball or
c. Second ball played under Rule 3-3 or Rule 20-7b in stroke play.

Note: Ball in play includes a ball substituted for the ball in play, whether or not such substitution is permitted.

15-1   GENERAL

A player must hole out with the ball played from the teeing ground unless a Rule permits him to substitute another ball. If a player substitutes another ball when not so permitted, that ball is not a wrong ball; it becomes the ball in play and, if the error is not corrected as provided in Rule 20-6, the player shall incur a penalty of loss of hole in match play or two strokes in stroke play.

15-2   MATCH PLAY

If a player plays a stroke with a wrong ball except in a hazard, he shall lose the hole.
If a player plays any strokes in a hazard with a wrong ball, there is no penalty. Strokes played in a hazard with a wrong ball do not count in the player's score. If the wrong ball belongs to another player, its owner shall place a ball on the spot from which the wrong ball was first played.

If the player and opponent exchange balls during the play of a hole, the first to play the wrong ball other than

from a hazard shall lose the hole; when this cannot be determined, the hole shall be played out with the balls exchanged.

15-3   STROKE PLAY

If a competitor plays a stroke or strokes with a wrong ball, he shall incur a penalty of two strokes, unless the only stroke or strokes played with such ball were played when it was in a hazard, in which case no penalty is incurred.

The competitor must correct his mistake by playing the correct ball. If he fails to correct his mistake before he plays a stroke from the next teeing ground or, in the case of the last hole of the round, fails to declare his intention to correct his mistake before leaving the putting green, he shall be disqualified.

Strokes played by a competitor with a wrong ball do not count in his score.

If the wrong ball belongs to another competitor, its owner shall place a ball on the spot from which the wrong ball was first played. (Lie of ball to be placed or replaced altered — see Rule 20-3b.)

RULE 18
BALL AT REST MOVED

Definitions:
A ball is deemed to have "moved" if it leaves its position and comes to rest in any other place.

An "outside agency" is any agency not part of the match or, in stroke play, not part of the competitor's side, and includes a referee, a marker, an observer and a forecaddie. Neither wind nor water is an outside agency.

"Equipment" is anything used, worn or carried by or for the player except any ball he has played at the hole being played and any small object, such as a coin or a tee, when used to mark the position of a ball or the extent of an area in which a ball is to be dropped. Equipment includes a golf cart, whether or not motorized. If such a cart is shared by two or more players, the cart and everything in it are deemed to be the equipment of the player whose ball is involved except that, when the cart is being moved by one of the players sharing it, the cart and everything in it are deemed to be that player's equipment.

Note: A ball played at the hole being played is equipment when it has been lifted and not put back into play.

A player has "addressed the ball" when he has taken his stance and has also grounded his club, except that in a hazard a player has addressed the ball when he has taken his stance.
Taking the "stance" consists in a player placing his feet in position for and preparatory to making a stroke.

18-1   BY OUTSIDE AGENCY

If a ball at rest is moved by an outside agency, the player shall incur no penalty and the ball shall be replaced before the player plays another stroke.

(Player's ball at rest moved by another ball—see Rule 18-5.)

18-2   BY PLAYER, PARTNER, CADDIE OR EQUIPMENT

a. General
When a player's ball is in play, if:
(i) the player, his partner or either of their caddies lifts or moves it, touches it purposely (except with a club in the act of addressing it) or causes it to move except as permitted by a Rule, or

(ii) equipment of the player or his partner causes the ball to move, the player shall incur a penalty stroke. The ball shall be replaced unless the movement of the ball occurs after the player has begun his swing and he does not discontinue his swing.

Under the Rules no penalty is incurred if a player accidentally causes his ball to move in the following circumstances:
In measuring to determine which ball farther from hole — Rule 10-4

In searching for covered ball in hazard or for ball in casual water, ground under repair, etc. — Rule 12-1

In the process of repairing hole plug or ball mark — Rule 16-1c

In the process of removing loose impediment on putting green — Rule 18-2c

In the process of lifting ball under a Rule — Rule 20-1
In the process of placing or replacing ball under a Rule — Rule 20-3a

In removal of movable obstruction — Rule 24-1.
b. Ball Moving After Address
If a player's ball in play moves after he has addressed it (other than as a result of a stroke), the player shall be deemed to have moved the ball and shall incur a penalty stroke. The player shall replace the ball unless the movement of the ball occurs after he has begun his swing and he does not discontinue his swing.

c. Ball Moving After Loose Impediment Touched
Through the green, if the ball moves after any loose impediment lying within a club-length of it has been touched by the player, his partner or either of their caddies and before the player has addressed it, the player shall be deemed to have moved the ball and shall incur a penalty stroke. The player shall replace the ball unless the movement of the ball occurs after he has begun his swing and he does not discontinue his swing.

On the putting green, if the ball or the ball-marker moves in the process of removing any loose impediment, the ball or the ball-marker shall be replaced. There is no penalty provided the movement of the ball or the ball-marker is directly attributable to the removal of the loose impediment. Otherwise, the player shall incur a penalty stroke under Rule 18-2a or 20-1.

18-3   BY OPPONENT, CADDIE OR EQUIPMENT IN MATCH PLAY

a. During Search
If, during search for a player's ball, the ball is moved by an opponent, his caddie or his equipment, no penalty is incurred and the player shall replace the ball.
b. Other Than During Search
If, other than during search for a ball, the ball is touched or moved by
an opponent, his caddie or his equipment, except as otherwise provided in the Rules, the opponent shall incur a penalty stroke. The player shall replace the ball. (Ball moved in measuring to determine which ball farther from the hole — see Rule 10-4.)
(Playing a wrong ball — see Rule 15-2.)

18-4   BY FELLOW-COMPETITOR, CADDIE OR EQUIPMENT

In Stroke Play
If a competitor's ball is moved by a fellow-competitor, his caddie or his equipment, no penalty is incurred. The competitor shall replace his ball. (Playing a wrong ball — see Rule 15-3.)

18-5   BY ANOTHER BALL

If a ball in play and at rest is moved by another ball in motion after a stroke, the moved ball shall be replaced.

Penalty for Breach of Rule
Match play: Loss of hole. Stroke play: Two strokes.

If a player who is required to replace a ball fails to do so, he shall incur the general penalty for breach of Rule 18 but no additional penalty under Rule 18 shall be applied.

Note 1: If a ball to be replaced under this Rule is not immediately recoverable, another ball may be substituted.

Note 2: If it is impossible to determine the spot on which a ball is to be placed, see Rule 20-3c.

RULE 19
BALL IN MOTION DEFLECTED OR STOPPED

Definitions:
An "outside agency" is any agency not part of the match or, in stroke play, not part of the competitor's side, and includes a referee, a marker, an observer and a forecaddie. Neither wind nor water is an outside agency.

"Equipment" is anything used, worn or carried by or for the player except any ball he has played at the hole being played and any small object, such as a coin or a tee, when used to mark the position of a ball or the extent of an area in which a ball is to be dropped.

Equipment includes a golf cart, whether or not motorized. If such a cart is shared by two or more players, the cart and everything in it are deemed to be the equipment of the player whose ball is involved except that, when the cart is being moved by one of the players sharing it, the cart and everything in it are deemed to be that player's equipment.

Note: A ball played at the hole being played is equipment when it has been lifted and not put back into play.

19-1   BY OUTSIDE AGENCY

If a ball in motion is accidentally deflected or stopped by any outside agency, it is a rub of the green, no penalty is incurred and the ball shall be played as it lies except:

a. If a ball in motion after a stroke other than on the putting green comes to rest in or on any moving or animate outside agency, the player shall, through the green or in a hazard, drop the ball, or on the putting green place the ball, as near as possible to the spot where the outside agency was when the ball came to rest in or on it, and

b. If a ball in motion after a stroke on the putting green is deflected or stopped by, or comes to rest in or on, any moving or animate outside agency except a worm or an insect, the stroke shall be cancelled, the ball replaced and the stroke replayed.

If the ball is not immediately recoverable, another ball may be substituted.

(Player's ball deflected or stopped by another ball — see Rule 19-5.)

Note: If the referee or the Committee determines that a player's ball has been purposely deflected or stopped by an outside agency, Rule 1-4 applies to the player. If the outside agency is a fellow-competitor or his caddie, Rule 1-2 applies to the fellow-competitor.

19-2   BY PLAYER, PARTNER, CADDIE OR EQUIPMENT

a. Match Play

If a player's ball is accidentally deflected or stopped by himself, his partner or either of their caddies or equipment, he shall lose the hole.

b. Stroke Play

If a competitor's ball is accidentally deflected or stopped by himself, his partner or either of their caddies or equipment, the competitor shall incur a penalty of two strokes. The ball shall be played as it lies, except when it comes to rest in or on the competitor's, his partner's or either of their caddies' clothes or equipment, in which case the competitor shall through the green or in a hazard drop the ball, or on the putting green place the ball, as near as

possible to where the article was when the ball came to rest in or on it.

Exception: Dropped ball — see Rule 20-2a. (Ball purposely deflected or stopped by player, partner or caddie — see Rule 1-2.)

19-3   BY OPPONENT, CADDIE OR EQUIPMENT

In Match Play
If a player's ball is accidentally deflected or stopped by an opponent, his caddie or his equipment, no penalty is incurred. The player may play the ball as it lies or, before another stroke is played by either side, cancel the stroke and play a ball without penalty as nearly as possible at the spot from which the original ball was last played (see Rule 20-5).

If the ball has come to rest in or on the opponent's or his caddie's clothes or equipment, the player may through the green or in a hazard drop the ball, or on the putting green place the ball, as near as possible to where the article was when the ball came to rest in or on it.

Exception: Ball striking person attending flagstick — see Rule 17-3b. (Ball purposely deflected or stopped by opponent or caddie — see Rule 1-2.)

19-4   BY FELLOW-COMPETITOR, CADDIE OR EQUIPMENT

In Stroke Play
See Rule 19-1 regarding ball deflected by outside agency.

19-5   BY ANOTHER BALL

a. At Rest
If a player's ball in motion after a stroke is deflected or stopped by a ball in play and at rest, the player shall play his ball as it lies. In match play, no penalty is incurred. In stroke play, there is no penalty unless both balls lay on the putting green prior to the stroke, in which case the player incurs a penalty of two strokes.

b. In Motion
If a player's ball in motion after a stroke is deflected or stopped by another ball in motion after a stroke, the player shall play his ball as it lies. There is no penalty unless the player was in breach of Rule 16-1g, in which case he shall incur the penalty for breach of that Rule.
Exception: If the player's ball is in motion after a stroke

on the putting green and the other ball in motion is an outside agency — see Rule 19-1b.

Penalty for Breach of Rule
Match play: Loss of hole.
Stroke play: Two strokes.

RULE 21
CLEANING BALL

A ball on the putting green may be cleaned when lifted under Rule 16-1b. Elsewhere, a ball may be cleaned when lifted except when it has been lifted:

a. To determine if it is unfit for play (Rule 5-3);

b. For identification (Rule 12-2), in which case it may be cleaned only to the extent necessary for identification; or

c. Because it is interfering with or assisting play (Rule 22).

If a player cleans his ball during play of a hole except as provided in this Rule, he shall incur a penalty of one stroke and the ball, if lifted, shall be replaced.

If a player who is required to replace a ball fails to do so, he shall incur the penalty for breach of Rule 20-3a, but no additional penalty under Rule 21 shall be applied.

Exception: If a player incurs a penalty for failing to act in accordance with Rule 5-3, 12-2 or 22, no additional penalty under Rule 21 shall be applied.

RULE 27
BALL LOST OR OUT OF BOUNDS

Provisional Ball
If the original ball is lost in an immovable obstruction (Rule 24-2) or under a condition covered by Rule 25-1 (casual water, ground under repair and certain damage to the course), the player may proceed under the applicable Rule. If the original ball is lost in a water hazard, the player shall proceed under Rule 26.

Such Rules may not be used unless there is reasonable evidence that the ball is lost in an immovable obstruction, under a condition covered by Rule 25-1 or in a water hazard.

Definitions:

A ball is "lost" if:

a. It is not found or identified as his by the player within five minutes after the player's side or his or their caddies have begun to search for it; or

b. The player has put another ball into play under the Rules, even though he may not have searched for the original ball; or

c. The player has played any stroke with a provisional ball from the place where the original ball is likely to be or from a point nearer the hole than that place, whereupon the provisional ball becomes the ball in play.

Time spent in playing a wrong ball is not counted in the five-minute period allowed for search.

"Out of bounds" is ground on which play is prohibited.

When out of bounds is defined by reference to stakes or a fence, or as being beyond stakes or a fence, the out of bounds line is determined by the nearest inside points of the stakes or fence posts at ground level excluding angled supports.

When out of bounds is defined by a line on the ground, the line itself is out of bounds.

The out of bounds line extends vertically upwards and downwards.

A ball is out of bounds when all of it lies out of bounds.

A player may stand out of bounds to play a ball lying within bounds.

A "provisional ball" is a ball played under Rule 27-2 for a ball which may be lost outside a water hazard or may be out of bounds.

27-1   BALL LOST OR OUT OF BOUNDS

If a ball is lost outside a water hazard or is out of bounds, the player shall play a ball, under penalty of one stroke, as nearly as possible at the spot from which the original ball was last played (see Rule 20-5).

Penalty for Breach of Rule 27-1
Match play: Loss of hole.
Stroke play: Two strokes.

27-2   PROVISIONAL BALL

a. Procedure

If a ball may be lost outside a water hazard or may be out of bounds, to save time the player may play another ball provisionally as nearly as possible at the spot from which the original ball was played (see Rule 20-5). The player shall inform his opponent in match play or his marker or a fellow-competitor in stroke play that he intends to play a provisional ball, and he shall play it before he or his partner goes forward to search for the original ball. If he fails to do so and plays another ball, such ball is not a provisional ball and becomes the ball in play under penalty of stroke and distance (Rule 27-1); the original ball is deemed to be lost.

b. When Provisional Ball Becomes Ball in Play

The player may play a provisional ball until he reaches the place where the original ball is likely to be. If he plays a stroke with the provisional ball from the place where the original ball is likely to be or from a point nearer the hole than that place, the original ball is deemed to be lost and the provisional ball becomes the ball in play under penalty of stroke and distance (Rule 27-1).

If the original ball is lost outside a water hazard or is out of bounds, the provisional ball becomes the ball in play, under penalty of stroke and distance (Rule 27-1).

c. When Provisional Ball to Be Abandoned

If the original ball is neither lost outside a water hazard nor out of bounds, the player shall abandon the provisional ball and continue play with the original ball. If he fails to do so, any further strokes played with the provisional ball shall constitute playing a wrong ball and the provisions of Rule 15 shall apply.

Note: If the original ball is in a water hazard, the player shall play the ball as it lies or proceed under Rule 26. If it is lost in a water hazard or unplayable, the player shall proceed under Rule 26 or 28, whichever is applicable.

RULE 28
BALL UNPLAYABLE

The player may declare his ball unplayable at any place on the course except when the ball is in a water hazard. The player is the sole judge as to whether his ball is unplayable.

If the player deems his ball to be unplayable, he shall, under penalty of one stroke:
a. Play a ball as nearly as possible at the spot from which the original ball was last played (see Rule 20-5); or
b. Drop a ball within two club-lengths of the spot where the ball lay, but not nearer the hole; or
c. Drop a ball behind the point where the ball lay, keeping that point directly between the hole and the spot on which the ball is dropped, with no limit to how far behind that point the ball may be dropped.

If the unplayable ball is in a bunker, the player may proceed under Clause a, b or c. If he elects to proceed under Clause b or c, a ball must be dropped in the bunker.

The ball may be cleaned when lifted under this Rule.

Penalty for Breach of Rule
Match play: Loss of hole.
Stroke play: Two strokes.

Appendix III

THE BALL

A. WEIGHT
The weight of the ball shall not be greater than 1.620 ounces avoirdupois (45.93 gm).

B. SIZE
The diameter of the ball shall be not less than 1.680 inches (42.67 mm). This specification will be satisfied if, under its own weight, a ball falls through a 1.680 inches diameter ring gauge in fewer than 25 out of 100 randomly selected positions, the test being carried out at a temperature of 23±1°C.

C. SPHERICAL SYMMETRY
The ball must not be designed, manufactured or intentionally modified to have properties which differ from those of a spherically symmetrical ball.

D. INITIAL VELOCITY
The velocity of the ball shall not be greater than 250 feet (76.2 m) per second when measured on apparatus approved by the United States Golf Association. A maximum tolerance of 2% will be allowed. The temperature of the ball when tested shall be 23±1°C.

E. OVERALL DISTANCE STANDARD
A brand of golf ball, when tested on apparatus approved by the USGA on the outdoor range at the USGA Headquarters under the conditions set forth in the Overall Distance Standard for golf balls on file with the USGA, shall not cover an average distance in carry and roll exceeding 280 yards (256 m) plus a tolerance of 6%.

Note: The 6% tolerance will be reduced to a minimum of 4% as test techniques are improved.

BIBLIOGRAPHY / CREDITS

500 Years of Golf Balls, History & Collector's Guide, John F. Hotchkiss, Antique Trader Books, 1997. *The Curious History of the Golf Ball, Mankind's Most Fascinating Sphere,* John Stuart Martin, Horizon Press, 1968. *The Glorious World of Golf,* Peter Dobereiner, The Ridge Press, Inc., McGraw-Hill Book Company, 1973. *A History of Golf, The Royal and Ancient Game,* Robert Browning, Ailsa, Inc., 1985. *The Story of American Golf,* Herbert Warren Wind, Alfred A. Knopf, Inc., 1975. *A History of Golf Illustrated,* Henry Cotton, J.B. Lippincott Company, 1975. *Golf's Magnificent Challenge,* Robert Trent Jones with Larry Dennis, Sammis Publishing Corp., McGraw-Hill Publishing Company, 1988. *The Encyclopedia of Golf Collectibles, A Collector's Identification and Value Guide,* John M. Olman and Morton W. Olman, Books Americana, Inc., 1985. *Golf Antiques & Other Treasures of the Game,* John M. Olman & Morton W. Olman, Market Street Press, 1993. *Strictly Golf Balls, The Golf Ball Handbook,* Revised Edition, Louis G. Caschera, Jr., StrictlyGolf, Inc., 1998. *Golf World Magazine,* December 17, 1999. *Golf Journal Magazine,* January/February, 2000.

www.usga.org — www.titleist.com — www.spalding.com— www.topflite.com — www.callawaygolf.com

ACKNOWLEDGEMENTS

A book depicting events of the past depends heavily on the memory and good nature of people who accurately recount those events and are willing to share them unselfishly. They become co-authors in effect. Larry Dennis and I, wish to thank all of you. It wasn't possible without you.

For significant help, we wish to thank: Dr. John Jepson, President, Noble Golf, Frank Thomas, Technical Director, U.S. Golf Association, John Spitzer, Assistant Technical Director, U.S. Golf Association, Dave Branon, President, Slazenger Golf USA, Jackie Beck, Marketing Communications Manager, Spalding, Mike Ferris, Category Management Director for Golf Balls, Spalding, Jim Butz, former president, PGA Victor Golf, Ken Devine, Executive Director, Michigan PGA Section, Tim Murphy, Editor, Golf World Business, Mike Johnson, Equipment/Special Projects Editor, Golf World Business and the National Golf Foundation.

For their encouragement and aid, I also want to thank: David Berkowitz who made his golf memorabilia collection available for photography, to Dr. Gary Wiren whose advice and ball collection were important to this book, to Jim Coit whose talents and good spirits are always appreciated, to Lew Fishman at Titleist R&D, to Jim Santy and Ron Muszalski at Cambridge Golf Antiquities, Ltd., and finally to my cat Olivia who tolerated me during this arduous, yet enjoyable, process.

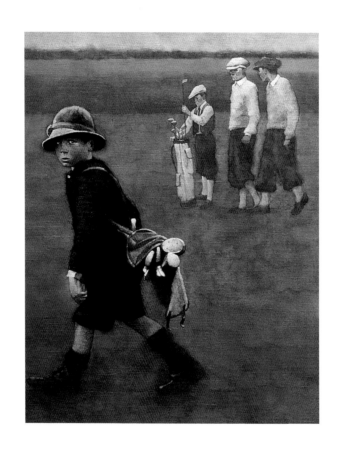